Contents

Stars of the Silent Era researched by **Jack Lodge**

Foreword

This book illustrates the story of the 'screen goddesses' from an unusual standpoint. In Japan, the popular movie magazine *Star* has built up over the years a remarkable archive of portraits and film stills; sent direct from the studios, many of these are dedicated personally to the magazine and its readers. Now released for wider appreciation, this splendid collection offers an intriguing journey through the American and European cinematic landscapes as viewed by another, very different culture. There are inevitable gaps – among film fans somebody essential always gets short measure in selections of this kind – but some at least of the missing faces have been restored without, we hope, disrupting the general emphasis and running order. The *Star* path takes some excitingly unfamiliar turns. But it confirms that the film world's marketing of its talents, incongruous and chauvinistic as such promotion can often be, maintains an enduring – and global – fascination.

The first film star, of course, was female: even before they knew her name, the international public began to look out for 'the Biograph Girl' and feel a special interest in any film which featured her. The label was known some time before the name, and was remembered long after the name was forgotten (for the record, it was Florence Lawrence). And already by 1910 she was considered such an asset that it was worth a rival producer's while to lure her away and engineer an elaborate deception about her alleged death in a streetcar accident just to garner extra publicity for the transformation of 'the Biograph Girl' into 'the IMP Girl'. In the process, the young lady's name came out, and the star system was born.

Not every star since Florence Lawrence has been female, certainly, but it was hardly by chance that it all started with a girl. Though in the nature of things screen romances needed as many heroes as heroines (and often more, since several men were frequently competing for one woman, but it was seldom that several women were competing for one man), and for every female-dominated weepie there was no doubt a male-dominated Western or war-film, the quintessential star was always a woman: Garbo rather than Gable, Crawford rather than Cooper, Monroe rather than Mastroianni. And this remains psychologically true even today, when, despite the complaints of feminists, men seem regularly to top the lists of box-office attractions in the cinema.

It is as though this pre-eminence as an image is to make up in some way for the relatively unimportant role women have tended until lately to play in the film-making process. Even that is partial and variable. In France, for example, most of the more prominent film-editors are women; in America, with a few honourable exceptions, this has not been so. In Hollywood women writers have generally been important; in Britain there have been relatively few to achieve prominence. But anywhere and everywhere, up to the end of the 1960s at least, women directors and producers have been exceptional enough to provoke comment, and when they have arrived at a position of such power – think of Nazimova, Leni Riefenstahl, Barbra Streisand – it has often been because they have won it through their fame and success in front of the camera.

Be that as it may, the film as a medium has been vitally involved with women, as product and as public, since its earliest days. And a vital part of this has always been the way they looked. Quite possibly modern theorists of sexual politics have a point when they insist that this was in general the result of stereotypes imposed by a male-dominated society. However, the simple criterion of whether a movie star was good to look at applied about as generally to men as to women on film, and since women bulked very large – were in fact for long regarded as the dominant force – in film audiences, it is difficult to believe that they had absolutely no say in the creation of their own image, or images.

As the *Star* collection amply demonstrates, there is an amazing diversity in the ways that women have actually looked on screen, even within any period of time short enough for fashions to remain reasonably constant. And this extends from the literal image to the metaphorical: though there is the occasional pin-up to give one the lie, the female film stars here depicted seldom seem to be on any level trapped in stereotypes, their own or anyone else's. Garbo was and remained a goddess, not because anyone else forced her to be so, but because of a certain mystery in her own temperament which the camera picked up as unerringly as the exquisite contours of the 'face of the century'. Joan Crawford was in every way a self-made woman, driven by an indomitable will which shaped the way she looked just as decisively as the roles she played. Marilyn Monroe had a love affair with the camera more potent that any she could have with a mere human being, and imposed her dream of herself upon the world. Mae West simultaneously created and destroyed her own image of womanhood in an ironic game which kept her audience, male and female, endlessly, enjoyably off-balance.

These were some of the stars, who might or might not be actresses as well. But there are also the actresses, those who constructed performances as others might make a painting or a sculpture. The cinema has always had room for them too, for all sizes and shades of personality and ability as well as for all types of beauty. What emerges from these images is not a circumscribed portrait of Woman as something apart, but a dazzling profusion of people who just happen, in all their infinite variety, to belong to the majority group in the Family of Man.

We invited Philip Strick, the distinguished critic and broadcaster, to respond to the *Star* collection with commentary and background information. He has done so with a connoisseur's enthusiasm. For Philip, as for so many film fans, a lifetime of film-going means that these faces are like family to him. He has the advantage of many of us, however, in that as well as having been a prolific writer and lecturer on film for 25 years, he has also been one of Britain's leading 16mm film distributors. He has been able to indulge his passion for movies by seeing them as often as he liked. His love of the cinema, supported by a formidable knowledge of its history, shines eloquently through his text. The *Star* goddesses could hardly ask for a more sympathetic admirer.

John Russell Taylor

PIN-UP PARADE

As soon as there were moving pictures, girls were a popular subject. They weren't the *only* subject – Muybridge was also known to study horses too – but they stirred the imagination and they brought in the customers. That's what showgirls, from the circus to the music-hall and theatre, had always been about, and the infant cinema had no other parents to learn from. So first came the peep-show parlours where it was said to be possible to glimpse forbidden secrets, and then, as the kinematograph gained in respectability, the scantily-clad Méliès ladies jostled with Bernhardt and Bertini for the limelight. In marketing Sarah Bernhardt's *Queen Elizabeth* in 1912 as 'Half a Mile of Rembrandt!', the industry smugly felt that it had discovered how to bring culture profitably to the masses. All it needed was 'Oomph'. Thus the pattern was established for shamelessly vulgar and blindly chauvinistic exploitation, in which the circulation of pin-ups fraught with promise played a vital role.

Burlesque versus Shakespeare. On balance, pioneer American showman Mack Sennett knew which he preferred. He saw the early slapstick comedies from France and assembled his own team of clowns to copy them. And if the Keystone Kops satisfied one market, the Mack Sennett Bathing Beauties, combining humour with kitsch, satisfied another. For a number of youngsters, they were also an important first step to a career spent before the camera.

Harriet Hammond *(b.1898)* gave up a musical career to join Sennett and went on to make romantic dramas like *Man and Maid* in the 1920s.

Marie Prevost *(1898-1937)* began with Sennett, later starred for Lubitsch in 1920s.

Annette Kellermann *(1888-1975)*, arrested in Boston in 1907 for wearing a one-piece bathing suit, starred in the sensational *Neptune's Daughter* (1914).

Phyllis Haver *(1899-1960)*, another successful Sennett star, later worked with Keaton, Griffith, Hawks, Ford, and De Mille.

Ann Dvorak *(1912-1979)*
Blithely posed on something
resembling an overgrown
cheesecake, Ann Dvorak plays the
studio game in peekaboo chiffon
for a publicity photo. A teenage
chorus girl in Charles Reisner's
The Hollywood Revue (1929), she
was at this time resuming her
screen career after a first film at
the age of three (Donald Crisp's
Ramona, 1916). From a showbiz
family, she had more talent than
the studios recognized at first, and
her expression shows it.

By 1932, she was being cast in
leading roles for Howard Hughes
(Sutherland's *Sky Devils* and
Hawks' *Scarface*), and the 1930s
were a busy and remunerative
time for her, culminating in being
directed by her then husband,
British actor Leslie Fenton, for
MGM's *Stronger than Desire*
(1939). For the next decade she
worked with just about everyone
from Flynn to Fonda to Cukor.
Then she gave up films in 1951 for
homes in Malibu and Honolulu, a
jet-set life of international travel,
and plenty to smile about.

Betty Grable *(1916-1973)*
Soaring above the ice-rink for a
photograph in 1939, Betty Grable
also looks as if she knows she's
heading for the heights. Her
career was just about to take off
after eight years of bit parts and
B-movie musicals in which she
was sometimes known as Frances
Dean. The famous legs, shortly to
be insured for fabulous sums, are
already in eye-catching form.

Lana Turner (b.1920)
Betty Grable's greatest competitor as top pin-up during the war years, Lana Turner exhibits customary poise in 1940. Her established image at the time was as the 'Sweater Girl', but here she adopts a wholesome open-air style which notably favours other aspects of her ensemble. The result is perhaps less flattering to her immaculate features and dazzling blonde hair, but the setting leaves no doubt that she's intent on the good life. Seven husbands did their best to help.

Susan Hayward (1918-1975)
Pinioned by a fallen parasol, Susan Hayward surrenders to catastrophe with the cover-girl nonchalance that first got her noticed. As a teenager, she modelled for the magazines until Cukor saw her on the front of *Saturday Evening Post*. By 1950, when this photo was taken, she'd already had the first of her five Oscar nominations and must have had her doubts about this kind of pose. Ever the professional, she doesn't let it show.

Danielle Darrieux *(b.1917)*
Twiddling an irrelevant leaf, the teenage Danielle Darrieux reveals several yards of leg with the innocent charm that made her the darling of pre-war French cinema. An international star by the age of 19, she had such regal elegance and looked so splendid in the frills and gowns of costume drama that while her daunting eyelashes and cool gaze have become welcome points of recognition, the rest of her is something of a surprise as though inexplicably overlooked and mislaid.

Rita Hayworth *(b.1918)*
At 13, she was a Spanish dancer in Mexican nightclubs. Four years later she signed up with Fox and there she is, pictured for the studio striking out on a new career as fun-loving outdoor girl with an intriguing resemblance to Greta Garbo. Stranded almost immediately, she was whisked into a contract with Columbia in 1937 by her first husband, and the sultry nightclub image closed profitably around her once more.

Sylvana Mangano (b.1930) in Giuseppe de Santis' *Bitter Rice* (1948).

Kim Novak (b.1933), dressed to kill in the mid-1950s.

Marina Vlady (b.1938); her 1950s films left little to the imagination.

Esther Williams (b.1923)
What Annette Kellermann
started, Esther Williams
continued. She was a swimming
champion by 15, and thanks both
to her looks and to her carefully-
trained acting and singing skills
she was soon recruited for the
movies, beginning inauspiciously
with *Andy Hardy's Double Life*
(George B. Seitz, 1942) but
quickly rising through the ranks.

At first a reluctant performer,
she was a major star by the late
1940s, and her underwater ballets
were among the most spectacular
of all MGM's musical sequences.
Her finest film, *Million Dollar
Mermaid* (Leroy, 1952) was the
story she had always wanted to
tell on screen – the biography of
Annette Kellermann, who at the
turn of the century had overcome
polio to become the world's first
great aquatic star.

By the 1950s nobody got
arrested for wearing one-piece
bathing suits any more – not even
Marina Vlady. But if Kellermann
had been prepared to scandalize,
Esther Williams never did. It was
convenient for her publicists that
she just happened to look
sensational in swimwear, but hers
was firmly a girl-next-door image,
all neat and self-contained in her
tiara on the way to the pool. For
less respectable considerations, it
was the Europeans like Sylvana
Mangano who seemed strangely
unable to stay inside their
clothing. The true American lady
was Esther Williams by day, Kim
Novak by night. Class stuff.
Nothing cheap.

15

Ava Gardner *(b. 1922)*
During the shooting of *The Little Hut* (Robson, 1957), Ava Gardner pauses for a photo-call. Her relationship with the camera lens was always something special. She'd had no acting experience whatever when MGM noticed her pictures in 1941, but the chemistry of the screen test was enough to win her a contract. Her debut film (which also marked Fred Zinnemann's debut as feature director and Van Heflin's as star) was *Kid Glove Killer* in 1942. But tailored to fit by the studio production line, she was almost anonymous in this and other such timefillers as *Three Men in White* (Goldbeck, 1944), a Dr Gillespie drama with Lionel Barrymore. In 1946, with Robert Siodmak's *The Killers*, the Gardner magic, with its lazy vulnerability, was at last revealed at full strength.

Gina Lollobrigida (b.1927)

Anita Ekberg (b.1931)

Anita Ekberg satirized the sex-bomb business in Fellini's *La Dolce Vita* (1960) and *Boccaccio 70* (1962), but remains typecast. An Oscar for *West Side Story* (Wise, 1961) released **Rita Moreno** from spitfire roles; now she's a feminist champion in television's *9 to 5*. For '**La Lollo**', the only way to beat the pin-ups was to become a photographer herself.

Rita Moreno (b.1931)

17

Ann-Margret (b. 1941)

Sylvia Kristel (b. 1952)

Samples of tepid erotica from the lemme-outa-here department. **Ann-Margret**'s legs have seldom appeared to worse advantage as her contemptuously seated companion chuckles after a garlic lunch. **Sylvia Kristel** sits in edgy disarray in her cane chair wondering where the cushion went. And **Jayne Mansfield**, sadly wasted except in Tashlin's *The Girl Can't Help It* (1956), twinkles for someone's identikit portrait of a dumb blonde.

Jayne Mansfield (1933-1967)

Raquel Welch *(b.1940)*
In Raquel Welch's career, it has taken some time for anyone to notice what she was saying. This didn't matter for *One Million Years BC* (Chaffey, 1966) when only grunting was necessary, but was just another disaster to add to *Myra Breckinridge* (Sarne, 1970).

In fact, given the chance and if anyone's listening, there are signs that Welch appeal can be more than skin-deep. As the gum-chewing rollerskate champion in *Kansas City Bomber* (Freedman, 1972), for example, or the terrified go-go dancer prey of a Los Angeles killer in *Flare Up* (Neilson, 1969), she provided good aggressive performances. But the worldwide ballyhoo that unleashed the Welch image on an incredulous public remains tough to transcend.

Still on the search for scripts requiring more of her than most would seek to ask, and meanwhile appearing on stage and television in her own song-and-dance shows, she is making the most of the aerobics craze by giving advice on body-building.

Ursula Andress (b.1936) fresh from the waves in Terence Young's *Dr No* (1962).

In Mack Sennett's day, the Bathing Beauties stood well back from the water. The idea was to pose, not to get soaked. Today's career girls have a different approach. In close touch with the elements, they emerge *from* the sea like a new life force, ready to fight for survival. From the decorative has evolved the decisive. Fortunately it remains photogenic.

Bo Derek (b.1957) at one with the ocean in Blake Edwards' '*10*' (1979).

STARS OF THE
SILENT ERA

Getting down to basics, we should start with the silent era. This section of the *Star* portrait gallery revives memories of some of the great screen personalities of the 1920s. The faces had a different look about them then. It wasn't just the hats, the hair, and the often startling plunges of neckline. It was the tiny, lipstick-sealed mouths. You can tell that the eyes had to do the talking. At a glance, a gaze, a flicker, or a glare, they could cause hearts to break. Some of these exquisite actresses were forced into retirement when sound came in, but the magic of their silence still lingers. Others, unjustly, are almost forgotten. But many of them continued in pictures after the coming of talkies. And amazingly, nearly all of them are in films which thanks to dedicated work by international archives can still be seen. Our guide through *Star*'s nostalgic cavalcade is silent movie specialist Jack Lodge, of the British Film Institute. He knows them well, some better than they knew themselves.

Mary Pickford

(1893-1979)

With William Haines in *Little Annie Rooney* (Beaudine, 1925).

In April 1909 at the Biograph studios in New York, film director D.W. Griffith engaged a young girl who was by now known as Mary Pickford. She was really Gladys Smith from Toronto, but stage producer David Belasco had invented a new, more distinguished name. For four years Mary made short films for Griffith and others, and soon became vastly popular as the 'Biograph Girl'. Many of those early mini-dramas like Griffith's *Wilful Peggy* (1910) and *The New York Hat* (1912) reveal an abundant charm, sincerity and skill. In 1913, she signed up with Famous Players for a series of feature films, and became the best known and highest paid ($10,000 a week in 1916) woman in the world.

Mary was an astute businesswoman, and achieved substantial control over her films. She also had fine directors like De Mille, Allan Dwan, and Maurice Tourneur – as well as Marshall Neilan, for whom she played an amazing dual role in *Stella Maris* (1918): the lovely invalid Stella, and the plain orphan Unity Blake. She intended that her films should be destroyed on her death, but gradually changed her mind, and her great 1920s features, with Charles Rosher's astonishing photography, still survive.

She didn't always play children, as the myth has it. Her parts were extremely varied, from the tomboy of the streets in Beaudine's *Little Annie Rooney* (1925) to the brave little protector of the orphans in Beaudine's marvellous *Sparrows* (1926), from the spirited working girl of *My Best Girl* (Lubitsch, 1927) and the fiery Kate of Sam Taylor's *The Taming of the Shrew* (1929) to the serene pioneer lady of Borzage's *Secrets* (1933), her last film and one of her finest. Few women in movie history have managed, like Mary Pickford, to combine super-stardom with such perfect artistry.

Fleeing through the Southern swamps in William Beaudine's *Sparrows* (1926).

The 'Big Four', founder-members of United Artists (1919): Douglas Fairbanks Sr (*left*), D.W. Griffith, Mary Pickford, Charles Chaplin.

22

Mabel Normand (1892-1930)

Edna Purviance (1894-1958)

Bebe Daniels (1901-1971)

Louise Fazenda (1895-1962)

Mabel Normand was one of the most gifted comediennes of the silent screen. She began in the early days at Biograph, went on to Sennett, starred with Chaplin in the first feature comedy, *Tillie's Punctured Romance* (1914), and was among the first woman directors.

The serene and gracious **Edna Purviance** was Chaplin's leading lady for nine years, with a final triumph in his first 'serious' film, *A Woman of Paris* (1923).

Eccentric **Louise Fazenda** was another Sennett comic, graduating to 1920s features like Raymond Griffith's *The Night Club* (1925) and an early Hawks, *The Cradle Snatchers* (1927).

In a long and versatile career, **Bebe Daniels** was Harold Lloyd's partner before moving on to De Mille and such dazzling comedies as *Why Change Your Wife?* (1920).

The great Russian dramatic actress, **Alla Nazimova**, came from the Broadway stage to the cinema in 1916, starred in the highly stylized *Salome* (1922), one of the most offbeat productions of the 1920s, and went on to character roles in such films as LeRoy's *Escape* (1940) and Mamoulian's *Blood and Sand* (1941).

Another stage star was **Pauline Frederick**, an adept at romantic melodrama, whose speciality was the ageing lady racked by a hopeless love, as in Lubitsch's *Three Women* (1924) and Clarence Brown's *Smouldering Fires* (1925).

Ruth Roland was a child actress who grew up to be a serial queen, second only to the legendary Pearl White.

Alla Nazimova (1879-1945), with 1922 film poster.

Ruth Roland (1892-1937)

Pauline Frederick (1883-1938)

Pina Menichelli (b.1893)

Anita Stewart (1895-1961)

Francesca Bertini (b.1892)

Pina Menichelli was one of the great stars of early Italian cinema. For some 12 years from around 1913, Menichelli, who never made a film outside Italy, incarnated a long series of *femmes fatales*, suffering and making her men suffer with her. Ahead of Theda Bara and others, she created in films like *Fire* (Fosco, 1914) the classic figure of the movie 'vamp'.

This was a period when half a dozen feminine stars dominated Italian movies, riding roughshod over directors, script and photography, and none was more regal than the dark and haughty **Francesca Bertini**, who played Juliet, Isolde, Camille, and almost every other sad heroine.

Anita Stewart was a Vitagraph star from 1911, formed her own production company a little later, and remained a leading name until sound came in. It is hard to see a Stewart feature nowadays, but early short films like *The Right*

Girl? (1915) and *His Phantom Sweetheart* (1915) reveal an actress of remarkable beauty and restrained skill.

Barbara La Marr was a tragic figure. She played exotic leads in the Hollywood 1920s – her best film was Ingram's *The Prisoner of Zenda* (1922) – was beautiful and immensely popular, but quite unable to adjust to the pressures involved. Before her death, from a drug overdose, at 29, she had been married six times and the subject of much scandal.

Another famous 1920s vamp was **Nita Naldi** (really Anita Dooley from New York), a dancer in the Ziegfeld Follies before her screen career began. Her first break was as a sultry dancer ensnaring John Barrymore in Robertson's *Dr Jekyll and Mr Hyde* (1920) and she was fascinating as the passionate Doña Sol opposite Valentino in Niblo's *Blood and Sand* (1922). But the 'vamp' was essentially a

creature of the silent movies. Words made her seem ludicrous, and Naldi's career, like those of many other wicked ladies, ended with sound.

But the supreme vamp was **Theda Bara**. The name was an anagram of 'Arab Death'; the lady was Theodosia Goodman, a tailor's daughter from Cincinnati, and so short-sighted that she could barely find her way about the set. Her stardom lasted some five years from 1915, but although that pale face and huge, staring eyes are familiar from stills, most of her films are lost, and tantalizing fragments of *A Fool There Was* (1915) are all one is likely to see of a girl who was a legend in her day.

Clara Kimball Young reached stardom in the Vitagraph days, and in 1914 a fan magazine poll placed her at the top in popularity. In 1915, she was an impressive Camille, and she became the

Nita Naldi (1909-1961)

Theda Bara (1890-1955)

Clara Kimball Young (1891-1960)

Barbara La Marr (1896-1926)

Constance Talmadge (1900-1973)

Mae Marsh (1895-1968)

Louise Brooks (b.1906) as Lulu in 1929.

leading actress of Lewis Selznick's World Films. In the 1920s, through her second husband's mismanagement of her career, the quality of her films deteriorated and she dropped from sight.

Constance Talmadge, younger sister of Norma, was a spirited comedienne whose career began with comedy shorts in 1914 and ended with the coming of sound. The sophisticated comedies like *Duchess of Buffalo* (1926) and *Venus of Venice* (1927) which made her almost as popular as her sister in the 1920s, have now vanished from sight, but Constance survives triumphantly with one performance: her portrayal of the Mountain Girl in *Intolerance* (1916) has a dynamic energy which matches the fury of Griffith's cutting.

Mae Marsh belongs to the immortals. The charm, sincerity and utter conviction of her roles in *The Birth of a Nation* and

Intolerance would guarantee that, but there was a long career ahead which included brief roles for John Ford – moments which still leap from the screen. She's there for just a glimpse in *The Grapes of Wrath* (1940) but that glimpse has the weight of film history behind it.

The strange career of **Louise Brooks** illustrates how the movies can destroy their own greatest talents. After some splendid roles in American silents, notably in Wellman's *Beggars of Life* (1925), she went to Germany for G.W. Pabst's *Pandora's Box* (1929), in which her Lulu, gleaming, irresistible and destructive, should have ensured her future. But after two more films in Europe, she could not readapt to Hollywood ways, and never had a real part again. Much later, her great films were rediscovered, and Brooks herself emerged as a writer, a shrewd

observer of the silent years.

Dorothy Gish was another girl with a more famous sister, but as with Norma and Constance Talmadge, Lillian and Dorothy were so dissimilar that there could be no family rivalry. Dorothy was at heart a comedienne, as she demonstrated in her role as the French girl with a comic walk in Griffith's *Hearts of the World* (1918), but she could shine in serious roles on occasion. In the 1915 *In Old Heidelberg*, a version of 'The Student Prince', she was a delight, and her blind girl in Griffith's epic *Orphans of the Storm* (1921) had both delicacy and pathos.

Few of **Alma Rubens'** films can now be seen (her last, Henry King's *She Goes to War*, 1929, is an exception), and she is remembered more for her unhappy personal life. By the mid-1920s she was a major star but a heroin addict and died aged 33.

Alma Rubens (1897-1931) with Gaston Glass in Borzage's Humoresque (1920).

Dorothy Gish (1898-1968)

The career of **Agnes Ayres** ended with the talkies, but she will always be remembered for her two romances with Valentino, *The Sheik* (1921) and *Son of the Sheik* (1926).

Billie Dove was a Ziegfeld showgirl before joining the movies. She was termed 'The American Beauty', which looked well-deserved in the Technicolor *The Black Pirate* (Parker, 1927).

Corinne Griffith, the 'orchid lady of the screen', is famous for the fact that in the 1960s, she claimed the real Corinne was dead and she was a stand-in.

Ethel Clayton, leading Lubin lady from around 1912, continued into the sound period; she was in the last Pickford film, *Secrets* (Borzage, 1933).

Alice Terry, one of the great silent actresses, was married to the director Rex Ingram, and appeared in *The Four Horsemen of the Apocalypse* (1921), *Scaramouche* (1923), and his masterpiece, *Mare Nostrum* (1926).

Irene Rich, who usually played women of the world, had her finest hour as Mrs Erlynne in Lubitsch's *Lady Windermere's Fan* (1925), but went on happily into sound films.

Blonde **Lila Lee** spent 20 years in films, was Valentino's leading lady in *Blood and Sand* (1922), and appeared successfully in sound films.

Mary Miles Minter, once a rival to Pickford, was the heroine of such notable films as *The Ghost of Rosie Taylor* (1918).

May McAvoy was Lubitsch's Lady Windermere in 1925, Ben-Hur's Esther in 1925, and the Jazz Singer's sweetheart in 1927.

Patsy Ruth Miller is remembered as Esmeralda in the Chaney *Hunchback* (1923),

Mary Philbin was Christine in Chaney's *Phantom of the Opera* (1925) and her marvellous performance here has seldom received its due.

Viola Dana played spirited leads in *The Cossack Whip* (1916), *Blue Jeans* (1917), and other films by her director husband John Collins.

Mildred Harris was an enchanting child actress, and then, for three years, the first wife of Charles Chaplin.

Madge Bellamy had also acted as a child, and went on in the 1920s to be the heroine of John Ford's *The Iron Horse* (1924).

Laura la Plante, a lively blonde, was in great silent thrillers like *The Cat and the Canary* (1927) and was Magnolia in the first *Show Boat* (Pollard, 1929).

Agnes Ayres (1896-1940)

Billie Dove (b.1901)

Ethel Clayton (1884-1966)

Corinne Griffith (1899-1979)

Irene Rich (b.1891)

Alice Terry (b.1900)

Lila Lee (1901-1973)

Mary Miles Minter (b.1902)

May McAvoy (b.1901)

Patsy Ruth Miller (1905-1981)

Viola Dana (b.1898)

Mildred Harris (1901-1944)

Mary Philbin (b.1903)

Madge Bellamy (b.1903)

Laura la Plante (b.1904)

Lois Moran (b.1908)

Carol Dempster (b.1902) with Neil Hamilton in D.W. Griffith's *America* (1924).

Colleen Moore (b.1902)

Janet Gaynor (b.1906) with George O'Brien in Murnau's *Sunrise* (1927).

Before making her Hollywood debut in 1925, **Lois Moran** from Pittsburgh had appeared in Marcel L'Herbier's classic film, *Feu Mathias Pascal* (1925). Her first Hollywood film was a classic too, Henry King's *Stella Dallas* (1926), in which she played the daughter, Laurel. But few good roles followed, and she retired in 1931.

Carol Dempster appeared almost exclusively in the films of D.W. Griffith, who was reputedly in love with her. A fine actress of considerable range, she could stand up to W.C. Fields in *Sally of the Sawdust* (1925), but was equally at home in a drama like *Isn't Life Wonderful?* (1924).

Colleen Moore, one of the most entrancing personalities of the silent years, was immensely and deservedly popular. Approaching 80, she was still zestful in the television series *Hollywood*. Particular Moore delights are *Ella Cinders* (1926), and *Twinkletoes* (1926), where she is an appealing Limehouse waif.

Janet Gaynor formed the most famous of all romantic partnerships in 12 films with Charles Farrell. With a wistful sweetness that was never cloying, she appeared within a single year in Borzage's *Seventh Heaven* (1927), *Street Angel* (1928), and Murnau's *Sunrise* (1927), winning the very first Best Actress Oscar.

Clara Bow (1905-1965), the 'It' girl of the 1920s with the cupid's-bow mouth.

Norma Shearer (1900-1983)

Bewitching was the word for **Clara Bow**. Changing times and styles have taken nothing away from her vibrant appeal, and her irresistible sense of fun; her great 1920s films, like Victor Fleming's *Mantrap* (1926) and *It* (Clarence Badger, 1927) are as fresh as on the day they were made. Whether she was playing a college girl, a shop assistant or a Red Cross nurse, she was warm, happy and lovely, and her characters had a tingling reality that leapt out of the screen. But her private life was touched by scandal, and she was plagued by nervous and physical ailments which brought about her retirement in the early 1930s.

In great contrast to Clara is the gentle and reserved **Norma Shearer**. Shearer's great days were in sound films of the 1930s, but she made some notable silents, playing anything from comedy to classics with equal assurance. In Victor Sjöström's *He Who Gets Slapped* (1924) she was the circus rider who captivates Lon Chaney's sad clown. In Monta Bell's *Upstage* (1926) she played a self-willed chorus-girl with notable honesty, and best of all was her touching little Kathi in Lubitsch's version of *The Student Prince* (1927). Her marriage to the head of MGM, Irving Thalberg, was no hindrance, but she clearly had talent enough to have got to the top without him.

Nathalie Kovanko (b.1899)

Lyla Mara (b.1897)

Nathalie Lissenko (1886?-1969)

Raquel Meller (1888-1962)

Nathalie Kovanko was in Russian films before the Revolution, and met and married the director Viatcheslav Tourjansky. After the Revolution the two emigrated to France, where Kovanko made many films during the 1920s, most of them under her husband's direction. Tourjansky directed *Michael Strogoff* in 1926 and was an assistant on Gance's *Napoléon* (1927); a studio photograph of the time shows Kovanko, darkly impressive under an enormous hat, sitting next to the great man.

Another star who worked mainly for her husband was the Polish **Lya Mara**, who appeared in German, Austrian and English films directed by Friedrich Zelnik, and for a few years in the 1920s was one of the leading actresses of the German cinema.

Nathalie Lissenko, from Russia, learned her craft under the great actor Mosjoukine. When she came to Paris, she was lucky indeed in her directors, working for Cavalcanti, Jean Epstein and Marcel L'Herbier, as well as for Mosjoukine himself in *Le Brasier Ardent* (1923), an excursion into fantasy which gave her a marvellous role.

Raquel Meller was a Spanish actress and singer, best remembered as Jacques Feyder's *Carmen* (1926). That performance is fierily impressive, but some say that Meller never equalled her earlier achievements with the director Henry-Roussell, who discovered her.

Lya de Putti, former dancer, worked with Lang and Murnau, played one of the most memorable of all vamp roles in Dupont's *Variety* (1925), spent two years in Hollywood, came to England for the first version of *The Informer* (1929), and died, tragically, of pneumonia at only 30.

Fern Andra was a New Yorker who became a star of German (and occasional British) silents. She can still be seen in Robert Wiene's *Genuine* (1920), giving a rather overheated performance in a very odd movie, and it is a pity that her films with the gifted Arthur von Gerlach are lost.

But **Lil Dagover** was in master works that survive. Overshadowed perhaps by the art direction in *Caligari* (1919), she was magnificent as the heroine caught between two worlds in Lang's *Destiny* (1921), and also in the first *Dr Mabuse* (1922). For Murnau, she was outstanding in *Phantom* (1922) and as Elmire in *Tartuffe* (1925). When sound came she displayed a caustic wit in *Der Kongress Tanzt* (1931) and was still acting shortly before her death in her 80s.

Henny Porten, the first great star of German cinema, was also lucky in her directors. She played *Anna Boleyn* for Lubitsch (1920), and in his *Kohlhiesel's Daughters* (1920) was both delightful and funny in a dual role as pretty and ugly sisters. There are effective performances from her in Leni's *Hintertreppe* (1921) and Dupont's *The Ancient Law* (1923). Her career effectively ended with the Nazi period.

Helena Makowska, a resplendent blonde beauty, was lured from the Warsaw stage to the early Italian studios, where they claimed never to have found anyone so photogenic. Her Italian work ranged from adventures with the muscle-man Maciste to Shakespeare, and later she worked successfully in German studios.

Maria Jacobini also worked in Italy and Germany, and was thought most un-Italian in her restrained style. She appears to have been a most moving *Anna Karenina* (1915).

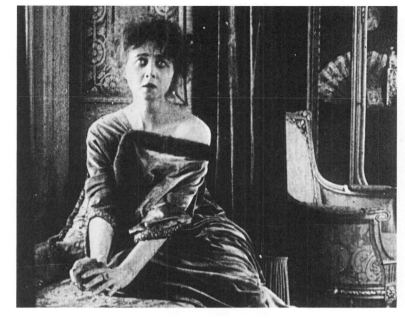

Helena Makowska (b.1895)

Maria Jacobini (1890-1944)

Lil Dagover (1897-1980)

Henny Porten (1888-1960)

Fern Andra (1893-1974)

Lya de Putti (1901-1931) seen, *left*, in Arthur Robison's *Manon Lescaut* (1926).

Pearl White (1889-1938)

In 1914 **Pearl White** starred in the mystery serial, *The Perils of Pauline,* and was soon one of the world's most popular stars. The following year, *The Exploits of Elaine* enhanced that popularity. She had been a circus rider until she suffered a spinal injury; then she was a film company secretary, enlisted one day for a part in a minor Western. Blonde, pretty and confident, she was an immediate hit. Only a few episodes of her serials survive, but they show her as spirited and natural; in spite of the injury, she did most of her own stunts.

Pola Negri was seen at her best in her German films. Dark and sensuous, yet always with a self-mocking humour, she played Carmen (1918) and Du Barry (1919) for Lubitsch, was a memorable spitfire in *Die Bergkatze* (1921) and in *Sumurun* (1920) an Arabian dancer who rouses the passion of a hunchback clown played by Lubitsch himself. When Negri went to Hollywood in 1923 she never quite found the roles to bring out her unique qualities. But she remained a striking personality, with a much publicized romance with Valentino, and marriages to a Count and to a Prince.

Dolores Del Rio's Latin beauty brought her a success in silent films from her debut in 1925, but she was seldom cast in other than ethnic roles, particularly when sound revealed her thickly accented speech.

Dolores Del Rio (1905-1983)

Pola Negri (b.1897) as Madame Du Barry with Emil Jannings in Lubitsch's *Passion* (1919).

Lois Wilson (b.1896) with J. Warren Kerrigan in James Cruze's *The Covered Wagon* (1923).

Greta Nissen (b.1906)

Vilma Banky (b.1903)
starred with Ronald Colman in
George Fitzmaurice's *The Night of Love* (1927).

Lois Wilson's film career began in 1916, when she played a small part in *The Dumb Girl of Portici*, the only film of the great ballerina Anna Pavlova. Through the 1920s she was in many major productions, most memorably *The Covered Wagon* (1923) and in *Monsieur Beaucaire* (1924) with Rudolph Valentino.

Blonde Norwegian **Greta Nissen** was a dancer who moved into films and became a notable player of sophisticated ladies like the carefree Parisienne who marries a desert chieftain in Howard Hawks' *Fazil* (1928). But she lost what could have been her most important role when her imperfect English caused her to be dropped from *Hell's Angels* in 1930 in favour of Jean Harlow.

Hungarian **Vilma Banky** moved from European films to Hollywood in the mid-1920s, and she and Ronald Colman were a popular romantic team, at their best in films like *The Winning of Barbara Worth* (1926). Banky also played opposite Valentino in *The Eagle* (1925), her performance blending nicely with the film's witty and ironic tone.

35

Gloria Swanson

(1899-1983)

Garbo-esque Swanson, early 1930s style.

Gloria Swanson was a glittering personality whose film career spanned 60 years. And she was usually rather bigger than her movies. Even in one of her early short comedies, *The Pullman Bride* (1917), her style and poise shine out from the tawdry material. Her best films were the smart comedies of romantic entanglement which she made for De Mille at Paramount in the early 1920s. She swept through them in a series of outrageous costumes, the epitome of outlandish glamour.

She married six times; once, in the 1920s, to a French Marquis and she and the studios enjoyed every moment of the publicity, with a band and a motorcade to welcome her home. When she moved into production on her own account, she hired Erich von Stroheim to make *Queen Kelly* (1928). But she became scared of

what Stroheim was doing, fired him, and issued a butchered parody of the film.

With sound, although her first talkie, *The Trespasser* (1929), was nominated for an Oscar, her status faltered. She came to England for *Perfect Understanding* (1933) with a very young Olivier, and seemed rather consciously to be trying to recover her youth. Then there was little until the triumph of Wilder's *Sunset Boulevard* (1950), where she gave one of the screen's supreme performances as the forgotten star with fantasies of a grand return. For Swanson the return was real – yet nothing she does in the film is finer than the great close-ups of her in *Queen Kelly*, which the screen Swanson watches with pride although the real Swanson had consigned them to oblivion. Egotistical she had been, but magnificent with it.

With Valentino in *Beyond the Rocks* (Sam Wood, 1922).

With Wally Albright Jr in Goulding's *The Trespasser* (1929).

With Myrna Loy (*left*) in *Airport 1975* (Smight, 1974).

Betty Compson (1897-1974), with Joseph J. Dowling and Thomas Meighan in George Loane Tucker's *the Miracle Man* (1919).

Fay Wray (b.1907)

Evelyn Brent (1899-1975)

Betty Compson was in mediocre items until George Loane Tucker's *The Miracle Man* (1919) made her a star overnight. She stayed at the top until the silents ended, a highlight being Sternberg's *The Docks of New York* (1928).

Sultry **Evelyn Brent** also owed her best roles to Sternberg, a spy in *The Last Command* (1928) and a gangster's moll in *Underworld* (1927). But she could be a good girl too, as in *Love 'Em and Leave 'Em* (1927).

Lovely **Esther Ralston**, a classic blonde, was in a small part in Lubitsch's masterpiece *The Marriage Circle* (1924), and was soon in Herbert Brenon's entrancing *Peter Pan* (1924).

The name of **Fay Wray** always evokes memories of *King Kong* (1933), but by then she had been in films for ten years; she reached stardom as the heroine of Stroheim's *The Wedding March* (1928).

Esther Ralston (b.1902)

Estelle Taylor (1899-1958)

Mary Astor (b.1906)

Lively brunette **Estelle Taylor** came from Broadway musicals to the screen in 1920, and for a few years was married to heavyweight champion Jack Dempsey. She played Miriam in De Mille's *The Ten Commandments* (1923), and Lucretia Borgia, opposite John Barrymore, in *Don Juan* (1926). Her sound films were rare, but included appearances for King Vidor in his *Street Scene* (1931) and for Jean Renoir in his *The Southerner* (1945).

Mary Astor was also in *Don Juan*, playing the nice girl to Taylor's villainess. That was one of her rare important silents. Famed for her role in Huston's *The Maltese Falcon* (1941), her finest films came in middle age, when she played cool, sophisticated ladies with charm and unshakeable poise.

Norma Talmadge, the one superstar of silent movies who failed almost completely to adapt to sound, began back in 1910 with Vitagraph and ended in 1930, when for *Du Barry, Woman of Passion* her Brooklyn accent was inappropriate. In between, she starred in countless romantic melodramas and occasional better roles with Frank Borzage (*Secrets*, 1924), and Clarence Brown (*Kiki*, 1926) who described her as 'the greatest pantomimist that ever drew breath'.

Norma Talmadge (1897-1957), with Arnold Kent in the silent film *The Woman Disputed* (1928) directed by Henry King and Sam Taylor, later released with a music and effects soundtrack.

THE 1930s

Fortunately for the cinema, strange as it seems, sound and the Depression arrived together. What spare cash the public had was devoted to the fascinating pastime of watching their idols talk. New directors and new writers of crisp and witty dialogue rendered Sennett's kind of comedy obsolete, and he was finally swept away in 1933 after the Wall Street crash. The films of the day were everything from Busby Berkeley to Little Caesar, from Karloff and Lugosi to Snow White. They were quick and inexpensive because they had to be, with the emphasis on basic skills like singing, dancing, and good plain acting. When the Hays Code, petty as it was, clamped down in 1934, it did the star system a world of good. Actresses who could convey the emotions without actually doing very much became a vital commodity. The fan magazines follow-ed every twist and turn in their lives, and what they wore influenced fashions around the globe. It was a good time to get into the movie busi-ness.

Greta Garbo

(b.1905)

Of all the icons in cinema legend, she remains the best known. To anyone, anywhere, her name evokes mystery, beauty, passion, anguish – and solitude. She had the power to rule Hollywood and the nerve to turn her back on it. She was an enigma; even the name was a mask, adapted by the Swedish director Mauritz Stiller in 1924 from a Hungarian monarch's name and a Spanish word meaning 'graceful'. She 'belonged' to Stiller, then to MGM, then to the public, then to John Gilbert, but finally to herself alone, retiring in 1941 after Cukor's *Two-Faced Woman*. There were indeed two faces of Garbo: the 'blank sheet of paper' (as Mamoulian said) on which her audience could write its own emotions: and the vulnerable face of a girl with faraway eyes – lost beyond recall.

Ernst Lubitsch's *Ninotchka* (1939) was promoted with the slogan 'Garbo Laughs!'.

With John Gilbert in Clarence Brown's *Flesh and the Devil* (1927).

With John Gilbert in Clarence Brown's *A Woman of Affairs* (1928).

As *Maria Walewska* (Brown, 1937), with Charles Boyer as Napoleon.

As *Anna Karenina* (Brown, 1935), with Fredric March.

As *Camille* (Cukor, 1936), with Robert Taylor.

As *Queen Christina* (1933), directed by Rouben Mamoulian.

Claudette Colbert

(b.1905)

Not surprisingly, her Cleopatra in 1934, sumptuously smothered by De Mille in plumes and golf leaf, was more Shaw than Shakespeare. She was an actress of wit and irony, able to throw away comic lines with a deadly accuracy. Competing with *Cleopatra* for the 1934 Oscars were two other Colbert films: the perennial weepie *Imitation of Life* (directed by John M. Stahl) and Capra's *It Happened One Night*, the comedy she hadn't been too keen to make. It was the comic role in Capra's film that won her the Award, and she became one of Hollywood's highest-paid stars.

In the films that followed there were plenty of comedies – classics like Lubitsch's *Bluebeard's Eighth Wife* (1938) and *Palm Beach Story* (1942) directed by Preston Sturges. In the 1950s, she turned to the stage, and later to television.

A very Merry Christmas from Claudette Colbert

In Frank Lloyd's *Maid of Salem* (1937).

With Bert Lahr in Cukor's *Zaza* (1939).

With Clark Gable in Frank
Capra's *It Happened One
Night* (1934).

With a teenage
Shirley Temple in
John Cromwell's *Since You
Went Away* (1944).

With Walter Pidgeon in Robert
Z. Leonard's *The Secret Heart*
(1946).

Marlene Dietrich

(b.1901)

When Joyce told her he admired *The Blue Angel*, she said 'You've seen the best of me', but in fact her best went into everything she did. Within seven years of the dizzy success of *Blue Angel* in 1930 she had been labelled 'box-office poison', but when George Marshall's *Destry Rides Again* was a hit in 1939 the Dietrich myth became unassailable. In the many films that followed (up to *Just a Gigolo* in 1979), she was more phenomenon than participant.

Despite the 17 films she'd made in Germany between 1919 and 1929, she claimed she was created by Josef von Sternberg, who discovered her on stage for Lola-Lola. He transplanted her to Hollywood, constructed around her such voluptuous visions as *Shanghai Express* (1932), *Blonde Venus* (1932) and *The Scarlet Empress* (1934), and left her after *The Devil is a Woman* in 1935. But if Sternberg was unique, there has also never been another Dietrich.

Sternberg's *Morocco* (1930) cast Dietrich as a cabaret girl in love with legionnaire Gary Cooper.

Her most famous role, as Lola-Lola in Sternberg's *The Blue Angel* (1930).

Sternberg's *Dishonoured* (1931), with Barry Norton.

Billy Wilder's *Witness for the Prosecution* (1957).

With Robert Donat in Feyder's *Knight Without Armour* (1937).

With Basil Rathbone in Boleslavsky's *The Garden of Allah* (1936).

Kay Francis

(1905-1968)

In 1929, after many stage appearances, she landed a tiny role with the Marx Brothers in *The Coconuts*. Then came a notable hit as the tremulously doomed heroine teamed up with William Powell as an escaped convict in Tay Garnett's *One Way Passage* (1932), and her career peaked in the late 1930s when she could be found with Errol Flynn in Dieterle's *Another Dawn* (1936) and Cary Grant in John Cromwell's *In Name Only* (1939). With her jet-black hair and intense, wide-set eyes, she made a menacing *femme fatale*. In the 1940s she produced her own films at Monogram before retiring once more to the stage.

Confessions (1937) directed by Joe May.

Standing back from the line of fire in George Marshall's *When the Daltons Rode* (1940).

Nancy Carroll

(1906-1965)

Born of Irish parents in New York, she trained as a dancer, making her stage debut at the age of 17. She became a theatre star, working with Lupino Lane in Hollywood, and a screen test led to her first film in 1927. It was Victor Fleming's *Abie's Irish Rose* (1928), in which she starred with Buddy Rogers, that made history: she was the first actress to sing and dance in a talkie feature. Nominated for an Oscar in 1930 for Edmund Goulding's *The Devil's Holiday*, she starred with all the best people in the 1930s but never, somehow, in the best films. In 1938, she went back to the stage.

Publicity shot, skating with Mickey Rooney, while working for MGM in the 1930s.

Miriam Hopkins

(1902-1972)

After starting as a chorus-girl she emerged a Broadway star in the 1920s and was spotted by Rouben Mamoulian. He teamed her with Fredric March for the third screen version of *Dr Jekyll and Mr Hyde* (1931), and launched both of them as major performers. But it was Lubitsch who brought out the authentic Miriam Hopkins with *The Smiling Lieutenant* (1931), *Trouble in Paradise* (1932), and *Design for Living* (1933), transforming her screen image from the conventional diminutive blonde required simply to look pretty, into a charming and manipulative schemer with a razor-sharp tongue and an intellect to match. The portrait of a woman firmly in charge of her emotions, her men, and her future suited Hopkins perfectly, and she maintained it through such dramas as King Vidor's *The Stranger's Return* (1933) and Mamoulian's *Becky Sharp* (1935). Then rivalries with Bette Davis in *The Old Maid* (Goulding, 1939) and *Old Acquaintance* (Sherman, 1943) led to her return to Broadway in 1943 with only occasional later film work, notably for Arthur Penn in *The Chase* (1966).

With Gary Cooper in Lubitsch's *Design for Living* (1933).

With Bette Davis in Vincent Sherman's *Old Acquaintance* (1943).

With Bing Crosby in *She Loves Me Not* (Nugent, 1934).

With Rex Harrison in Victor Saville's *Storm in a Teacup* (1937).

With Fredric March in Mamoulian's *Dr Jekyll and Mr Hyde* (1931).

With Brian Donlevy and Edward G. Robinson in Hawks' *Barbary Coast* (1935).

Sylvia Sidney

(b.1910)

Whenever there was trouble, Sylvia Sidney seemed to get the worst of it in the 1930s. One of the screen's most frequent victims to the inconstant male, her sweetly tormented features always come to mind from Hitchcock's *Sabotage* (1936), where she struggled with the bearish Oscar Homolka, from Fritz Lang's *Fury* (1936) with the bullish Spencer Tracy, or Frank Lloyd's *Blood on the Sun* (1945) with the extravagant Cagney.

There was no shortage of such roles when she reached the screen in the 1920s after a Broadway debut at 15, but eventually she tired of them and returned to the stage in the 1940s until the character parts got interesting. It was a sensible decision, leading in due course to her Oscar nomination for *Summer Wishes, Winter Dreams* (Gilbert Cates, 1973) and a nice cameo in Wenders' *Hammett* (1982).

With Gary Cooper in Mamoulian's *City Streets* (1931).

With Fredric March in Gering's *Good Girl* (1934).

With Cary Grant in Gering's *Madame Butterfly* (1932).

Janet Gaynor
(b.1906)

She began as an extra, but a successful screen test for Fox in 1924 resulted in her quickly becoming known as 'the World's Sweetheart', and after the popular series of films with Charles Farrell she was the first actress in screen history to win an Oscar (in 1928). She made a painless transition to sound pictures, began the 1930s as America's top star, refused to marry Charles Farrell despite the urging of their many fans (he was, after all, already married), and charmed her way through a fine variety of movies until, with savings of well over a million dollars, she announced her retirement after making *The Young in Heart* in 1938. Together with *Seventh Heaven* (1927) it was her favourite film, but there had been other successes along the way such as the William Wellman version of *A Star is Born* which won her an Oscar nomination in 1937.

She had a radiant simplicity that made her the natural choice for country-girl roles, but she was also an astute business woman and although she refuses any further limelight she has retained a powerful influence in Hollywood circles.

With Douglas Fairbanks Jr and Paulette Goddard (*right*) in Richard Wallace's *The Young in Heart* (1938).

With Henry Fonda (his debut) in Victor Fleming's *The Farmer Takes a Wife* (1935).

Joan Crawford

(1904-1977)

One of the cinema's great monuments. After at least 19 films in the silent era, bulldozing her way up from bit parts to female lead in low-budget quickies, she was a star in 1928 as the jazz-baby in Harry Beaumont's *Our Dancing Daughters* – all plunge neckline, daringly short hair, and pearls. In the 1930s, the hardly-disputed queen of MGM, she matured magnificently through an average of three films a year, some of them less than suitable like *Rain* or *The Gorgeous Hussy* (Clarence Brown, 1936), others simply requiring that she look superb while men fell at her feet.

The favourite Crawford images, though, come from later work – the Oscar-winning *Mildred Pierce* (Curtiz, 1945), the gunslinging, piano-playing saloon keeper of *Johnny Guitar*, the tattered recluse of *Whatever Happened to Baby Jane?* (Aldrich, 1962).

In Nicholas Ray's *Johnny Guitar* (1954).

With Walter Huston in Lewis Milestone's *Rain* (1932).

Myrna Loy

(b. 1905)

Together, she and William Powell made the perfect team. Both had heavy eyelids, bodies needing furniture for support, voices that spoke in riddles, hands only reassured by a full glass. As the Thin Man husband-and-wife unit they were the indolent, indulgent, Thorne-Smith-crazy kind, absurd, degenerate, and terribly enviable.

Typecast as a slinky Oriental after joining Grauman's Chinese Theatre at 18, memorable in support of Karloff for the Brabin/Vidor *Mask of Fu Manchu* (1932), Myrna graduated as Mrs Nick Charles to become 'Queen of the Movies', but abdicated gracefully to the Red Cross during the war. She returned resoundingly in Wyler's *The Best Years of Our Lives* (1946), and maintained an elegant profile into the 1970s.

With Clark Gable in Victor Fleming's *Test Pilot* (1938).

With William Powell and Asta the dog in *The Thin Man* (W.S. Van Dyke, 1934).

Jean Harlow

(1911-1937)

The bombshell image of the screen meant nothing but trouble in her private life. It was a brief and sensational career, beginning in 1926 when at 15 she became a film extra (getting the Laurel and Hardy treatment in *Double Whoopee* in 1928), became an overnight scandal in Howard Hughes' *Hell's Angels* (1930) which enraged moralists across the States, and established her reckless good-time gal reputation with *Public Enemy* (Wellman, 1931) and *Platinum Blonde* (Capra, 1931). Then came the partnership with Gable for, among others, Victor Fleming's smouldering *Red Dust* (1932), a dozen films for MGM in four years, a turbulent and highly public affair with William Powell, and fatal illness at 26.

Beside Clark Gable in Sam Wood's *Hold Your Man* (1933).

As showgirl with French flying ace Cary Grant in *Suzy* (Fitzmaurice, 1936).

With Robert Taylor in W.S. Van Dyke's *Personal Property* (1937), her last film.

Barbara Stanwyck

(b.1907)

An orphan, at 13 she worked in a store, then at the Ziegfeld Follies. At 19, she was on Broadway, at 20 in Hollywood. In 1982, she received an honorary Oscar. She could act anyone else straight off the screen.

With Burt Lancaster in *Sorry, Wrong Number* (Litvak, 1948).

With Fred MacMurray in Billy Wilder's *Double Indemnity* (1944).

Jeanette MacDonald

(1901-1965)

In the 1920s she sang in Broadway musicals like *Irene*. When musicals came to Hollywood, so did she. She was fun, she was lovely, and her voice was enchanting. With MGM co-star Nelson Eddy, she sang on for 20 sentimental years.

With Ray Bolger in *Sweethearts* (W.S. Van Dyke, 1938).

In her first film, *The Love Parade* (Lubitsch, 1929) with Maurice Chevalier.

Ginger Rogers

(b.1911)

She danced from amateur Charleston contests to Broadway musicals to Hollywood in 1930, beginning her ten-year partnership with Astaire in *Flying Down to Rio* (Freeland, 1933). She could sing and act, too, winning her Oscar in 1941 with Sam Wood's *Kitty Foyle*, and proving a marvellous comedienne in, for example, Hawks' *Monkey Business* (1952). Back on Broadway in the 1960s and 1970s, she continues light on her feet.

Studio shot of Ginger with Ralph Bellamy and Fred Astaire preparing for *Carefree* (Sandrich, 1938).

With Astaire in George Stevens' *Swing Time* (1936).

Ginger and Fred in H.C. Potter's *The Story of Vernon and Irene Castle* (1939).

With Joseph Cotten in the war-time love-story *I'll Be Seeing You* (Dieterle, 1944).

Grace Moore

(1901-1947)

Her parents had other plans, but all she ever wanted to do was sing, disappearing to Greenwich Village cafés at an early age to do so. After studying music in Paris, she won a contract with the help of Irving Berlin to the Metropolitan Opera Company. MGM liked her voice, and her popularity with opera lovers was enough to put her in two 1930 productions, Franklin's *A Lady's Morals* and the Romberg-Hammerstein operetta *New Moon* (director, Jack Conway). But they didn't care for her increasing waistline, and it was for Columbia that she achieved her greatest hit, *One Night of Love* (Schertzinger, 1934).

In parallel with Jeanette MacDonald, she developed the public taste for operatic movies in the 1930s; her effervescent charm also promised a successful future as an actress, but a plane crash tragically intervened.

Scenes from *When You're in Love* (1937), co-directed by Harry Lachman and Capra's dialogue writer Robert Riskin, (*left*) with Cary Grant.

Jean Parker

(b.1915)

Awarded an MGM contract after a couple of years on stage, pretty teenager Jean Parker patiently submitted to the horrors of studio grooming and sweet-young-thing roles in a large number of 1930s films. Beginning with a Jackie Cooper tearjerker *Divorce in the Family* (Reisner, 1932), she rose to better prospects in La Cava's much-praised *Gabriel Over the White House* (1933), Cukor's *Little Women* (1933) and René Clair's *The Ghost Goes West* (1935), and was starred with Boyer, Robert Taylor and others in a few minor programme-fillers. Nothing much else happened but Laurel and Hardy (*The Flying Deuces*, 1939), so she recovered her independence and went back to the stage, with only selective later screen appearances.

Game for anything in daft publicity photo (Jean's the bunny on the left).

Taking note of Boyer in *Caravan* (Charrell, 1934).

Jean Arthur

(b.1908)

She was in more than 20 silent films, mostly comedies and Westerns, and when the talkies arrived she still tended to be on a horse or wise-cracking or both. Her first major hit was in Ford's *The Whole Town's Talking* (1935), followed by plenty of leading roles as the resourceful action-packed Calamity Jane type in classic Capra comedies. The tough stuff, she claims, is all a façade: shy in real life, she retired after *Shane* and became a college lecturer in drama and film.

With Cary Grant in Hawks' *Only Angels Have Wings* (1939); *(right)* with Cesar Romero, Edward Arnold in *Diamond Jim* (Sutherland, 1935).

With Gary Cooper in De Mille's *The Plainsman* (1936).

With Charles Boyer (*centre*) in Borzage's *History is Made at Night* (1937).

With Alan Ladd and Van Heflin in George Stevens' *Shane* (1953).

Carole Lombard

(1908-1942)

Greatest of the 'screwball' heroines, she began with Mack Sennett after a tomboy role in Allan Dwan's *A Perfect Crime* (1921). With her delightful beauty and her miraculous sense of timing, she was launched by Hawks' *Twentieth Century* in 1934 on a wonderful succession of hits like *My Man Godfrey* (La Cava, 1936), *Nothing Sacred* (1937), Hitchcock's under-rated *Mr and Mrs Smith* (1941), and Lubitsch's *To Be Or Not To Be* (1942). Killed in a plane crash at 34, she remains mourned by millions.

A sample of Lombard elegance.

With James Stewart in *Made for Each Other* (Cromwell, 1939).

With husband William Powell in *Man of the World* (Wallace, 1931).

With Fred MacMurray on the set of *The Princess Comes Across* (Howard, 1936).

As Hazel Flagg, toast of New York, in Wellman's *Nothing Sacred* (1937), with reporter Fredric March.

Loretta Young

(b. 1913)

You wouldn't say her films made history, but what she gave them was warmth and a touch of class. A child star, she was just 15 at the time of *Laugh, Clown, Laugh* (Brenon, 1928) in which Lon Chaney was her admirer, and there were other successes in *Platinum Blonde* (Capra, 1931) and *The Farmer's Daughter* (1947) for which she won an Oscar.

In 1953 she left cinema for television, becoming hostess of the Loretta Young Show.

Grass-skirted for publicity in the 1930s.

With Joseph Cotten in *The Farmer's Daughter* (Potter, 1947).

Olivia de Havilland

(b.1916)

With Clark Gable in *Gone With the Wind* (Fleming, 1939).

It fell to Olivia to deliver the lines most cherished by bad-movie buffs everywhere: 'There's a swarm of killer bees heading this way. . .' That was in Irwin Allen's *The Swarm* (1978) in which she was a schoolmarm being courted by Ben Johnson and Fred MacMurray. Olivia could always rise above that sort of thing; even when coping with Sonny Tufts in *Government Girl* (Nichols, 1943) she was able to dismiss the ludicrous and the just plain dull with a pyrotechnic display of expressions and gestures. What suited her best, as *Gone With the Wind* illustrated to everybody's satisfaction, were gracious roles with a hint of the sinister – the mental patient in *The Snake Pit* (Litvak, 1948), or the Oscar-winning *To Each His Own* (Leisen, 1946) and Wyler's *The Heiress* (1949).

From the mid-1950s she made only the occasional return to the big screen. In 1982 she played the Queen Mother in a television film.

In a double role (spot the join) with Lew Ayres in Siodmak's *The Dark Mirror* (1946).

Deanna Durbin

(b.1921)

With Gene Kelly in *Christmas Holiday* (Siodmak, 1944).

With Melvyn Douglas in *That Certain Age* (Ludwig, 1938).

At 15 in 1936, she made a short for MGM, *Every Sunday*, co-starring Judy Garland. When MGM decided to keep Judy but not Deanna, it was Universal's gain; from her very first starring role, *Three Smart Girls* (Koster, 1937), the radiant teenager was a huge hit. She had a remarkable soprano voice, a wide repertoire of light classics, and she was wholesome – as *100 Men and a Girl, Mad About Music* (Taurog, 1938), and *Three Smart Girls Grow Up* (Koster, 1939) charmingly illustrated.

When Deanna *did* grow up, of course (her last film was *Lady on a Train* in 1945, directed by the man she married, Charles David), late-starter Judy Garland was there to take over.

With Adolphe Menjou, Mischa Auer, in *100 Men and a Girl* (Koster, 1937).

Shirley Temple

(b.1928)

With dancing lessons at the age of two, she started early. She needed to; she was in movies a couple of years later in a series called Baby Burlesks. Among other activities in these mini-tot satires, she impersonated Dietrich. Singing at six in *Stand Up and Cheer* (1934) she was such a hit that they gave her a larger role in *Little Miss Marker* (Hall, 1934) and she was well away. She won a special Oscar in 1934, just for being Shirley Temple, and popped up in 20 films over four years.

If the truth be told, she was far more presentable as a teenager, and her performances in Cromwell's *Since You Went Away* (1944) and *Fort Apache* (Ford, 1947) are worth anyone's time and respect. But it was curls and dimples the fans wanted, so she went into politics instead.

Nine-year-old Shirley in John Ford's *Wee Willie Winkie* (1937).

Nineteen-year-old Shirley with Myrna Loy in Irving Reis' *The Bachelor and the Bobbysoxer* (1947).

Norma Shearer (1900-1983) won a total of five Oscar nominations, and received the Award for *The Divorcee* (Leonard, 1930). Wife of MGM boss Irving Thalberg, she could command the best parts and was known in the mid-1930s as the 'First Lady of MGM'. Thalberg planned *Marie Antoinette* (pictured here) for her but died two years before it was made by W.S. Van Dyke in 1938.

Ann Harding (1902-1981) was RKO's silver-blonde leading lady in the 1930s. She was usually cast as the wronged but noble wife, always loyal to the end.

Tallulah Bankhead (1902-1968) came from a wealthy and influential background, specialized in the 'rich bitch' role, but could act too (witness Hitchcock's *Lifeboat*, 1944).

Ruth Chatterton *(1893-1961)*, glossy star who sandwiched a ten-year movie career between her Broadway hits, was popular in generally mediocre films. Shown here in *Journal of a Crime* (1934), directed by William Keighley.

Eleanor Powell *(1912-1982)* was a spectacular tap-dancer from an early age. Partnered with Fred Astaire in *Born to Dance* (1936) and *Broadway Melody of 1940* she won the ultimate accolade when Astaire said she could outdance even him. From 1943 she was known as Mrs Glenn Ford.

Constance Cummings *(b. 1910)* made 20 films in the 1930s, but her first loyalty was to the stage. Memorable as Harold Lloyd's champion in *Movie Crazy* (Bruckman, 1932) and with Rex Harrison in Lean's *Blithe Spirit* (1945).

Constance Bennett *(1906-1965)* was a hit in Cukor's *What Price Hollywood?* (1932), but she made her fortune in the business world and acting was just a profitable sideline.

Ethel Barrymore *(1879-1959)* was never entirely happy away from the stage but was marvellous on celluloid. Her Oscar was for *None But the Lonely Heart* (Odets, 1945). Here with Laughton in Hitchcock's *The Paradine Case* (1947).

Joan Bennett *(b. 1910)* worked with all the best directors, including Cukor, Borzage, Lang, Ophuls, and Minnelli. Shown here in *Little Women* (Cukor, 1933) with (from left on sofa) Frances Dee, Katharine Hepburn, Jean Parker.

Anita Louise (b.1915) spent most of the 1930s looking decorative in costume films like *Madame Du Barry* (1934), *A Midsummer Night's Dream* (1935), and *Marie Antoinette* (1938). Her last film was *Retreat, Hell!* (1952) for director Joseph H. Lewis, after which she enjoyed a happier career on television and as a fund-raiser for charities.

Joan Blondell (1909-1979) could be guaranteed to walk off brightly with any film she appeared in, everything from *Public Enemy* (1931) to *Grease* (Kleiser, 1978). With her unfailing sparkle, even minor character roles were given life, substance, and a warm sense of fun.

Mae West

(1892-1980)

She made her stage debut at five as 'The Baby Vamp', and the image of outrageous prodigy stayed with her through years of burlesque, vaudeville and revue. Famous for her one-liners, the talent for innuendo she brought to her scripts was all her own, the sex-goddess parody entirely her own construction. As a night-club star she had to be seen to be believed, and the movies never really did her justice – particularly as censorship took the sting out of them for the first three. But experiences like *I'm No Angel* (Ruggles, 1933) and *Klondike Annie* (Walsh, 1936), based on her own play, remain without equal for their blissful vulgarity.

With W.C. Fields in *My Little Chickadee* (Cline, 1940).

A typical pose, festooned with plumes, from 1932. Her eyes perpetually addressed the gods, who loved her for it.

Jean Muir *(b.1911)* was a magical Helena in Reinhardt's *A Midsummer Night's Dream* (1935). She was in films from 1933 for ten years, but the stage was her real home.

Marie Dressler *(1869-1934)* starred for Sennett, fell to obscurity, returned in bit parts for MGM in the late 1920s, won an Oscar for George Hill's *Min and Bill* in 1930, and her death was greatly mourned throughout the USA.

Gertrude Michael *(1911-1964)* went from Broadway to Paramount as the polished leading lady of minor films, with smaller roles in many major movies (she was Calpurnia in De Mille's *Cleopatra* in 1934).

Dorothy Jordan *(b.1908)* was a Broadway dancer before going to Hollywood for the Pickford-Fairbanks *Taming of the Shrew* (Taylor, 1929). Best known for her appearances in John Ford films of the 1950s.

Françoise Rosay

(1891-1974)

From the Comédie Française, she made her first screen appearance in 1913, worked with husband Jacques Feyder in Hollywood in 1928, and became a star when they returned to France with her rousing performances in *Le Grand Jeu* (1933) and *La Kermesse Héroique* (1935), both directed by Feyder. After the war she pursued an international career – in Britain, Dearden's *The Halfway House* (1944) and *Saraband for Dead Lovers* (1948); in the States, *The Sound and the Fury* (Ritt, 1959). A much-loved celebrity in France, she worked constantly in the theatre.

In her most famous role in *La Kermesse Héroique* (1935).

With Pierre Richard-Willm in Feyder's *Le Grand Jeu* (1933), the film which inspired *Vertigo*.

As hotel-owner in love with her adopted son in Feyder's *Pension Mimosas* (1934).

As night-club boss in Marcel Carné's *Jenny* (1936).

With Marie Bell in Duvivier's *Un Carnet de Bal* (1937).

Annabella

(b. 1909)

She began her screen career at 18 as the inn-keeper's daughter Violine who catches Napoleon's eye in Abel Gance's epic *Napoléon* (1927). Then the two films she made for René Clair, *Le Million* (1931) and *Quatorze Juillet* (1932) made her a leading star and suddenly she was everywhere. She was in Britain's first Technicolor production *Wings of the Morning* (Schuster, 1937) with Henry Fonda, and in Victor Sjöström's *Under the Red Robe* (1937) with Conrad Veidt, and then it was an easy step to Hollywood for *Suez* (Dwan, 1938) and marriage to Tyrone Power. After an unhappy decade in the States she returned to France, and retired in 1953.

With René Lefèvre in Clair's *Le Million* (1931).

In René Clair's *Quatorze Juillet* (1932).

With Jean Gabin in Julien Duvivier's *La Bandéra* (1935).

With Pierre Richard-Willm in Raymond Bernard's *Anne Marie* (1936).

Marie Bell

(b.1900)

Another recruit from the Comédie Française, she appeared in silent films from 1924 (the first was René Hervil's *Paris*) and played leading roles for Feyder, Duvivier (notably *Un Carnet de Bal*, 1937), and many others during the 1930s.

Active in the Resistance during the war, she gave up the cinema in the 1940s but was tempted back for *La Bonne Soupe* (Thomas, 1964), *Vaghe Stelle dell'Orsa* (Visconti, 1965), and *Hotel Paradiso* (Glenville, 1966).

With Jean Murat in Epstein's *L'Homme à l'Hispano* (1933).

With Pierre Richard-Willm in Feyder's *Le Grand Jeu* (1933).

Edwige Feuillère

(b.1907)

She graduated from the Paris
Conservatoire in 1931 and made
the theatre her home, hailed as a
new Bernhardt. The first films
were undistinguished but after her
theatrical partnership with
Barrault she became a force to be
reckoned with – in L'Herbier's
L'Honorable Cathérine (1942) and
Cocteau's *L'Aigle à Deux Têtes*
(1947). Her perfect features and
troubled eyes made her an ideal
heroine for Max Ophüls in *Sans
Lendemain* (1939) and *Sarajevo*
(1940).

As the ferocious school-teacher in Jacqueline
Audry's *Olivia* (1951).

With Fernand Gravey in Robert Siodmak's *Mister Flow* (1936).

81

Madeleine Renaud

(b.1903)

Joining the Comédie Française in 1921, she made her first film the following year at 19. Both versatile and appealing, she had no difficulty making the switch to sound; in 1931, in two films directed by Harry Lachman, she showed she could be a tragic wife (*La Belle Marinière*) or a society flirt (*La Couturière de Lunéville*) with equal skill. Playing a penniless student, she starred with her husband Jean-Louis Barrault in his first film *Les Beaux Jours* (1935), and together they founded their famous repertory company in Paris in 1946.

With Jean-Louis Barrault in *Les Beaux Jours* (1935).

Viviane Romance

(b.1912)

A teenage star of the music-halls, she was popular throughout the 1930s for her smouldering screen portrayals of temptresses, vamps, and good-time girls of all description. Gorgeous in costume, menacing in nightgown, she relieved men of their wealth without much argument in such films as Mathot's *Manon 326* (1932), Grémillon's *L'Etrange Monsieur Victor* (1938), and Duvivier's famous *Pépé le Moko* (1936). She retired in the 1960s, but returned in a welcome cameo in Chabrol's *Nada* (1973).

With Jean Gabin in Julien Duvivier's *La Belle Equipe* (1936).

In Raymond Bernard's *Maya* (1949), which she produced herself.

Danielle Darrieux

(b.1917)

One of the most enchanting ladies of French cinema, she has enjoyed a wide-ranging international career which started in 1931 when she was 14. Guided by film-maker Henri Decoin (whom she later married) through a number of popular comedies in the 1930s, she found instant fame for her doomed partnership with Charles Boyer in *Mayerling* (Litvak, 1936), and the flow of successes has never stopped since. Among them, a trio of classics for Ophüls in the 1950s, Broadway in the 1970s, and Demy's musical chiller *Une Chambre en Ville* in 1982.

With Anton Walbrook in *Port Arthur* (Falkas, 1935).

With Charles Boyer in Anatole Litvak's *Mayerling* (1936).

In Henry Koster's *The Rage of Paris* (1938).

With Erno Crisa in Allégret's *L'Amant de Lady Chatterley* (1955).

With Gérard Philipe in Autant-Lara's *Le Rouge et le Noir* (1954).

With Vittorio de Sica in Max Ophüls' *Madame De …* (1953).

Lilian Harvey

(1906-1968)

British, but educated in Berlin, she was a chorus-dancer in a revue when her first film role came along in 1925. The talkies revealed her command of languages and her delightful singing voice and she became widely popular; but it was in Germany, in a series of musicals with her husband Willy Fritsch, that she really became a cult figure.

In the comedy *Ihr Dunkler Punkt* (1928).

In Erik Charrell's *Der Kongress Tanzt* (1931), with Conrad Veidt, Henri Garat.

In *Der Kongress Tanzt*, which she made in English, French and German.

Simone Simon

(b.1914)

Best known for her sinister,
sinuous ambiguity in Val Lewton's
1940s productions, she had the
good luck to work with some other
greats as well: Borzage for
Seventh Heaven (1937), Renoir for
La Bête Humaine (1938), and
Ophüls for *La Ronde* (1950). She
gave up cinema, more's the pity,
in the mid-1950s.

With Kent Smith in Jacques Tourneur's *Cat People* (1942).

With Jean-Pierre Aumont in Marc Allégret's *Lac aux Dames* (1934).

Trude von Molo (b.1909) was an intriguing German star of the 1930s, coming to the cinema after light opera in Vienna. Shown here in Curtis Bernhardt's *Der Mann der den Mord Beging* (1931).

Gaby Morlay (1893-1964) made her movie debut in 1914, alternating between supporting roles on stage and on film. Shown here with Boyer in Marcel L'Herbier's *Le Bonheur* (1934).

Marta Eggerth (b.1912) was a star of Austro-Hungarian operetta in the 1930s with her husband, the famous tenor Jan Kiepura. She appeared in Douglas Sirk's musicals of 1936, *Das Hofkonzert* and *La Chanson*.

Dorothea Wieck (b.1908) was a pupil of Max Reinhardt, won recognition in Leontine Sagan's *Mädchen in Uniform* (shown at the first Venice Festival in 1932), but was unsuccessful in Hollywood and returned to German studios in the mid-1930s.

Corinne Luchaire (1921-1950) was a hit in Leonide Moguy's *Prison sans Barreaux* (1938) and Pierre Chenal's *Le Dernier Tournant* (1939) but was accused of being a collaborator during the war; her career never recovered.

Elisabeth Bergner (b.1900) mainly appeared in films by husband Paul Czinner (beginning with *Nju*, 1924), worked in Britain and Hollywood after 1933 (notably *Catherine the Great*, 1934), and was still filming in her eighties.

Olga Tschechowa (1896-1980), Chekhov's niece, was both film-maker and star in the 1920s and 1930s, working for F.W. Murnau, Clair, E.A. Dupont (*Moulin Rouge*, 1928), Henrik Galeen, and Ophüls (*Liebelei*, 1932).

Paula Wesseley *(b.1908)* became one of the most prolific German stars of the 1930s after her enchanting performance in actor-director Willi Forst's *Maskerade* (1934).

Brigitte Helm *(b.1906)* was Lang's famous robot in *Metropolis* (1926) and found herself typecast as heartless temptresses. She retired in 1935 after nine silent, 16 sound films.

Franciska Gaal *(b.1909)* went from European cabaret to Hollywood roles for De Mille (*The Buccaneer*, 1938) and MGM (Taurog's *The Girl Downstairs*, 1939), and was briefly hailed as another Mary Pickford.

Zarah Leander *(1900-1981)* made her first films in Sweden but found stardom in 1937 in Douglas Sirk's German operetta films *Zu Neuen Ufern* (*To New Shores*) and *La Habanera*.

THE 1940s

The war could have brought out the best in Hollywood, supporting the war effort, showing the folks back home what heroism was all about, and helping them to pick up the pieces when the fighting stopped. But one look at the pictures shows it wasn't like that at all. There was certainly some propaganda cinema, and Churchill said *Mrs Miniver* was worth a fleet of battleships, but as the overseas market was largely demolished the Hollywood policy was to pretend the war wasn't happening. They rushed out a mass of cheaply-made escapist films that took audiences' minds off their troubles. It was only later, during the Cold War, that a kind of nostalgia became apparent for the simple good-versus-evil values of personal sacrifice, and battlefield heroism became cinematic spectacle. By the end of the 1940s, after strikes, blacklisting, a crippling overseas tax – and television – the movie business wasn't looking too healthy. The gals of the pin-ups and the musicals were about all it had left.

Katharine Hepburn

(b.1907)

Like her hair and the erratic cadences of her voice, she follows no established pattern, picks no conventional path through dialogue or drama. Her screen appearances could be termed eccentric were they not, more importantly, so sane, so controlled and all-conquering. Although she played the headstrong girl in many of the early films for RKO, the Hepburn image seems always to have had the authority of a distant, slightly shocking, older relative – an unexpected aunt, say, who would find it the most natural thing in the world to torpedo a Nazi boat on an African lake, or take to the skies on a great balloon adventure.

With her fierce, no-nonsense beauty and her imperturbable sense of humour she will always be the cinema's most seductive illustration of the advantages of independence.

With (*from left*) Frances Dee, Joan Bennett, Jean Parker in George Cukor's *Little Women* (1933).

With Robert Walker in *Song of Love* (Brown, 1947).

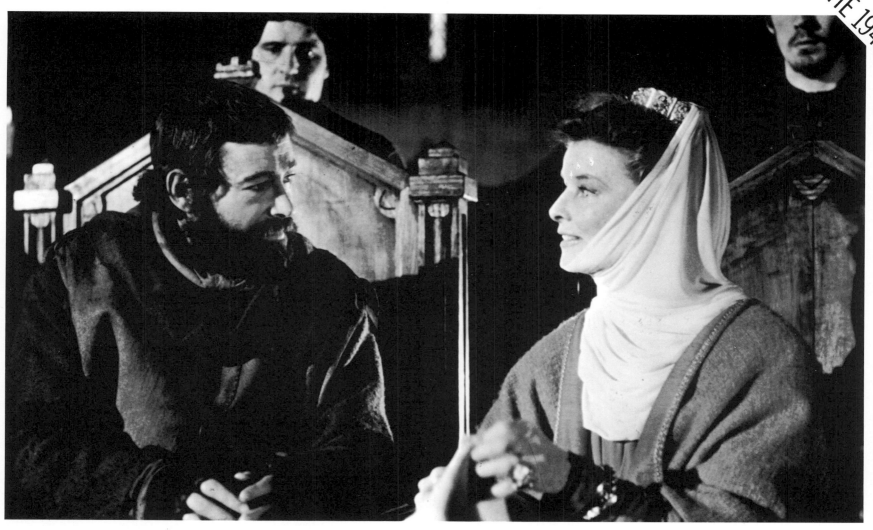

In her Oscar-winning role as Eleanor of Aquitaine in *The Lion in Winter* (Harvey, 1968), with Peter O'Toole.

As the tourist who falls in love in Venice in David Lean's *Summertime* (1955).

With Burt Lancaster in *The Rainmaker* (Anthony, 1956).

Winning another Oscar in *Guess Who's Coming to Dinner* (Kramer, 1967), with Spencer Tracy.

93

Bette Davis

(b.1903)

She arrived in Hollywood in 1930, and they grappled with each other from then on. 'There wasn't one of my best pictures,' she claims, 'I didn't have to fight to get.' Partly it was the eyes which, at a flicker, dispensed a lethal distaste. Partly it was the voice, which cracked and whined like a whip. And partly it was the personality which cared nothing for studio glamour, but demanded respect and scripts that were intelligent. And now, with two Oscars, ten nominations, an Emmy Award, and some of the finest films ever made to her credit, she bears the scars of her 50-year battle with an amiable pride. Nobody's about to dispute her victory.

With Leslie Howard in Archie Mayo's *The Petrified Forest* (1936).

With Herbert Marshall in Wyler's *The Little Foxes* (1941).

With Mary Astor in Edmund Goulding's *The Great Lie* (1941).

With Paul Henreid in *Now Voyager* (Rapper, 1942).

With Marilyn Monroe and George Sanders in Mankiewicz's *All About Eve* (1950).

In Irving Rapper's *Deception* (1946).

In Robert Aldrich's *Whatever Happened to Baby Jane?* (1962).

Irene Dunne

(b.1904)

You always felt she could solve any problem instantly in her head, but for courtesy would give her men the chance to talk it through for themselves until they got it right. Once she was going to be an opera singer, but the New York Metropolitan turned her down so she was in musical comedy for eight years until a tour with *Show Boat* won her an RKO contract in 1930. Not surprisingly, *Show Boat* was intended as an early film project, but by the time it was made – by James Whale in 1936 – Irene's popularity had already been resoundingly established in no less than 19 movies, including versions of *Cimarron* (Ruggles, 1931), *Back Street* (Stahl, 1932)

With Randolph Scott in *High, Wide and Handsome* (Mamoulian, 1937).

and *Magnificent Obsession* (Stahl, 1935) that still outshine the remakes.

Her first two (of five) Oscar nominations came for *Theodora Goes Wild* (Boleslavsky, 1936) and McCarey's *The Awful Truth* (1937), and by the 1940s she was approaching the status of a national institution in such classics as *The White Cliffs of Dover* (Clarence Brown, 1944), *Anna and the King of Siam* (Cromwell, 1946), and George Stevens' *I Remember Mama* (1948). After the role of Queen Victoria in *The Mudlark* (Negulesco, 1950), she took the only logical remaining step, entered politics, and became a delegate at the United Nations.

In characteristic pose at the grand piano in John Cromwell's *This Man is Mine* (1934).

With Robert Taylor in John M. Stahl's *Magnificent Obsession* (1935).

With Rex Harrison in John Cromwell's *Anna and the King of Siam* (1946).

With Philip Dorn in George Stevens' *I Remember Mama* (1948).

Joan Fontaine

(b.1917)

Born in Tokyo like her older sister Olivia de Havilland – from whom she stole the Oscar for *Suspicion* (1941) and thus began a bitter feud – she was the more brittle and self-effacing of the two.

Uninspired by wallpaper roles in the 1930s, she was on the point of quitting when *Rebecca* (Hitchcock, 1940) arrived by accident, an Oscar nomination resulted, and she found more juicy roles on offer, like *Jane Eyre* (Stevenson, 1944) with Orson Welles. The 1940s were good years, peaking with Ophüls' *Letter from an Unknown Woman* (1948) and Nicholas Ray's *Born to be Bad* (1950). Eighteen movies later, and after 1967 she settled for the occasional television role.

With Isabel Jeans (*left*) in Hitchcock's *Suspicion* (1941).

With Richard Haydn and Bing Crosby in Billy Wilder's *The Emperor Waltz* (1948).

With Ray Milland in George Stevens' *Something to Live For* (1952).

With Laurence Olivier and Judith Anderson in Hitchcock's Oscar-winning *Rebecca* (1940).

Greer Garson

(b. 1908)

Every inch a lady, she was spotted by the head of MGM on a West End stage in 1938 and got the role of Robert Donat's wife in Sam Wood's *Goodbye Mr Chips* (1939). Nominated for an Oscar, from then on she played valiant, saintly spouses like Wyler's *Mrs Miniver* (1942), which won her both an Oscar and a husband, and LeRoy's *Madame Curie* (1944). She then tried some new approaches, including a bubble-bath in Conway's *Julia Misbehaves* (1948), settled for the usual formula in *The Miniver Story* (Potter, 1950), and then went back to the theatre.

With Ronald Colman in Mervyn LeRoy's *Random Harvest* (1942).

With Walter Pidgeon in Wyler's *Mrs Miniver* (1942).

With Walter Pidgeon and Margaret O'Brien in *Madame Curie* (LeRoy, 1944).

With Lionel Barrymore in *The Valley of Decision* (Garnett, 1945).

As Calpurnia in Mankiewicz's *Julius Caesar* (1953), with Louis Calhern, Marlon Brando.

Rita Hayworth

(b.1918)

Like the racehorses with which her name became associated she was a beautiful mover, and there could be a hint of scandal just in the way she lit a cigarette. Although the marriages got more press than the movies, both contributed to the 'love goddess' image that made her fortune in the 1940s. In the hands of Hawks for *Only Angels Have Wings* (1940), Charles Vidor for her most famous role in *Gilda* (1946), or Welles for the unforgettable *Lady from Shanghai* (1947), she showed that she could act, too.

With Glenn Ford in *The Loves of Carmen* (Vidor, 1948)..

Also with Glenn Ford in Charles Vidor's *Gilda* (1946).

Lana Turner

(b.1920)

With never a hair out of place, she was less classy than Rita Hayworth in her choice of films, but outclassed even Rita when it came to romantic adventures. For a good dozen years her statistics were so widely displayed that every movie she was in drew the crowds. Nothing much else about them, however, was worth watching until the 1950s, when Minnelli and Sirk really made the most of her in *The Bad and the Beautiful* (1952) and *Imitation of Life* (1959).

(Right) with Clark Gable in Jack Conway's *Honky Tonk* (1941).

With Gable in *Betrayed* (Reinhardt, 1954).

With Fernando Lamas in *The Merry Widow* (Bernhardt, 1952).

103

Jennifer Jones

(b.1919)

Notorious for her 'lust in the dust' image, created as much by the constantly rapacious expression as by down-to-earth roles of passion in King Vidor's *Duel in the Sun* (1946) and *Ruby Gentry* (1952), she was in fact more often the well-manicured madam, notably in John Huston's remarkable *We Were Strangers* (1949) or the Theodore Dreiser heroine *Carrie*, filmed by William Wyler in 1952. Her Oscar was for the saintly *Song of Bernadette* (King, 1943), for which Selznick groomed her prior to their 16-year marriage.

With Laurence Olivier in Wyler's *Carrie* (1952).

In Vittorio de Sica's *Indiscretion of an American Wife* (1953).

With William Holden in *Love is a Many Splendoured Thing* (King, 1955).

Virginia Mayo

(b.1920)

Ballet dancer, then straight woman to a performing horse in vaudeville, she could cope with just about anything and tended, on the strength of a Goldwyn contract, to get Bob Hope (Butler's *The Princess and the Pirate*, 1944) and Danny Kaye (McLeod's *Secret Life of Walter Mitty*, 1947). Beautiful, with a touch of venom, she was a popular pin-up but deserved better movies than they ever found for her.

With Joel McCrea in *Colorado Territory* (Walsh, 1949).

With Danny Kaye in *The Kid from Brooklyn* (McLeod, 1946).

Dorothy Lamour

(b. 1914)

Typecast as a beauty of the South Seas, she was so popular in the 1940s that two Lamour sarongs auctioned for war bonds fetched $2 million. From shop-girl to beauty contest queen to hotel singer to radio to Hollywood, she started her cinematic world tour as *The Jungle Princess* (Thiele, 1936), and was on the road with Crosby and Hope by 1940. A more enjoyable fellow-traveller would be hard to imagine.

With Irene Dunne and Randolph Scott in Rouben Mamoulian's *High, Wide and Handsome* (1937)

With Henry Fonda and George Raft in Henry Hathaway's *Spawn of the North* (1938).

With Bob Hope and Bing Crosby on the *Road to Utopia* (Walker, 1944).

Betty Grable

(1916-1973)

Once she got to Fox in 1940, the undistinguished earlier films were forgotten and she became the favourite G.I. pin-up and, briefly, Hollywood's highest-paid star. Strangely, the films didn't improve – there are few fond memories today for such musicals as *Sweet Rosie O'Grady* (Cummings, 1943), *Pin-Up Girl* (Humberstone, 1944), or *Mother Wore Tights* (Lang, 1947) – and in the mid-1950s, eclipsed by Monroe (they starred together in Negulesco's *How to Marry a Millionaire*, 1953), she took up a stage career.

With Cesar Romero in Irving Cummings' *Springtime in the Rockies* (1943).

Teresa Wright

(b.1918)

Her unemphatic, reliably loyal image is probably best recalled from Hitchcock's *Shadow of a Doubt* (1943), but her Oscar was for the supporting role in Wyler's *Mrs Miniver* (1942). That she could also be headstrong and tough was shown by her performance as Mitchum's girl in the Raoul Walsh Western *Pursued* (1947).

Still filming in the 1970s, she was a welcome visitor to *Roseland* (Ivory, 1977) and to *Somewhere in Time* (Szwarc, 1980). She also continues with stage and television work.

With Fredric March and Myrna Loy (*seated*) in William Wyler's *The Best Years of Our Lives* (1946).

Paulette Goddard

(b.1911)

The girl with the sparkling grin, who after her first wealthy marriage at 16 went on to wed Chaplin, Burgess Meredith, and the writer Erich Maria Remarque, very nearly became Scarlett O'Hara. Instead, her screen fame largely derives from *Modern Times* (1936) and *The Great Dictator* (1940), although she was equally enchanting in *The Cat and the Canary* (Nugent, 1939), Cukor's *The Women* (1939), *So Proudly We Hail* (Sandwich, 1943), Mitchell Leisen's *Kitty* (1945), and Renoir's *Diary of a Chambermaid* (1946). Later films like *Bride of Vengeance* (Leisen, 1949) and *Babes in Baghdad* (Ulmer, 1952) were less reputable, and she retired to enjoy the wealthy life in the mid-1950s.

With Chaplin in *The Great Dictator* (1940)

With Gary Cooper and director Cecil B. De Mille for *Unconquered* (1947).

Janis Paige (b.1923)

Priscilla Lane (b.1917) with sisters Rosemary, (Gale Page as fourth 'sister') and Lola, on set for Curtiz's *Four Daughters* (1938).

A smashing redhead, **Janis Paige** always had better luck with stage than screen until television provided her with the series *It's Always Jan* in the 1950s. Never quite getting the star roles, she could be glimpsed in George Sidney's *Bathing Beauty* (her first film, 1944), and seen to advantage in *Of Human Bondage* (Goulding, 1946) and *Cheyenne* (Walsh, 1947). She did better with MGM for Mamoulian's *Silk Stockings* (1957) and a succession of bright comedies in the 1960s.

Singer and comedienne with a Pennsylvania danceband at the age of 14, **Priscilla Lane** appeared with the band in *Varsity Show* (Keighley, 1937) and teamed with two of her sisters for *Four Daughters*. This prompted a successful series of family pictures which enabled her at the same time to build up a solo career. She was particularly notable in Robert Rossen's *Blues in the Night* (1941) and as Cary Grant's wife in *Arsenic and Old Lace* (Capra, 1944). After a total of 23 films she retired in 1948.

From the film of her Broadway success, *Claudia* (Goulding, 1943), **Dorothy McGuire** launched into a 33-year movie career, her gentle but determined features particularly memorable for Siodmak's haunting terror-film *The Spiral Staircase* (1945), in which she was the killer's mute prey, and for Wyler's *Friendly Persuasion* (1956), as the Quaker wife struggling to keep her family out of the Civil War. Seen here (*top*) discovering Rhonda Fleming's body and suspecting Gordon Oliver in *The Spiral Staircase*.

Dorothy McGuire (b.1918) with James Dunn and Lloyd Nolan in Kazan's *A Tree Grows in Brooklyn* (1945).

Rosalind Russell (1908-1976) went from Broadway to MGM in 1934, equally at ease in melodrama or comedy. Shown here (*top*) as *Auntie Mame* (Da Costa, 1958) and with Jane Wyman at a 1948 première.

Jane Wyman (b.1914), the former Mrs Reagan (*top*), was in 40 films before achieving stardom in the mid-1940s and an Oscar for *Johnny Belinda* (Negulesco, 1948); (*above*) with Richard Carlson in *The Blue Veil* (Bernhardt, 1951).

Betty Hutton (*b.1921*), vivacious Paramount musical star of the 1940s, hit her peak with *Annie Get Your Gun* (Sidney, 1950) with Howard Keel (*top*) but hard times were to come. (*Above*) in *Perils of Pauline* (Marshall, 1947).

Lucille Ball (*b.1911*), fashion-model with RKO contract in the 1930s, became one of the world's best-loved comediennes. Seen here (*top*) with Red Skelton in Del Ruth's *Dubarry Was a Lady* (1943). She also launched the very successful television series *I Love Lucy*.

Anne Baxter *(b. 1923)*, intriguing Oscar-winner for Edmund Goulding's *The Razor's Edge* (1946), worked with Welles, Wilder and Hitchcock, gave it all up for sheep-farming, but reappeared in the 1970s. Seen here with Bette Davis and Gary Merrill in Mankiewicz's *All About Eve* (1950).

Linda Darnell *(1923-1965)*, promoted by Fox as 'the girl with the perfect face', starred in Tyrone Power movies and classics (*above*) like Ford's *My Darling Clementine* (1946), and Preminger's *Forever Amber* (1947), but failed in cabaret in the 1950s.

Piled high with furs or stripped down to tatters, **Gene Tierney** had a sultry, enigmatic style that caught the eye. Although it was probably Preminger's *Laura* (1944) that left the most lasting impression, she was a formidable *Belle Starr* (Cummings, 1941), brooded darkly in Hathaway's *Sundown* (1941) and Ford's *Tobacco Road* (1941), turned to comedy with Lubitsch's *Heaven Can Wait* (1943), and gained an Oscar nomination as Cornel Wilde's moody, petulant wife in *Leave Her to Heaven* (Stahl, 1946).

Gene Tierney (b.1920)

In the RKO musicals of the late 1930s, a dancing brunette would appear for a couple of numbers and leave the rest of the movie in the shade. It was thanks to Lucille Ball's support that the exuberant teenager **Ann Miller** was recruited by RKO for such fillers as *The Life of the Party* (Seiter, 1937) and *Radio City Revels* (Stoloff/Santley, 1938), and she was soon taken up by MGM to become a vital component of the 'golden age' of musicals. Partnered by Fred Astaire in *Easter Parade* (Walters, 1948) she was also memorable in *On the Town* (Kelly/Donen, 1949), *Lovely to Look At* (LeRoy, 1952), and *Kiss Me Kate* (Sidney, 1953). She continued her career into the 1970s on stage and in television.

Ann Miller (b.1924)

Margaret O'Brien (b.1937) on screen from the age of four, won her Oscar in Minnelli's *Meet Me in St Louis* (1944). After LeRoy's *Little Women* (1949) with Janet Leigh, June Allyson, Elizabeth Taylor (*above*), with teenage roles the magic slipped away.

Claire Trevor (b.1909) with John Wayne in John Ford's *Stagecoach* (1939). She won Oscar nominations in Wyler's *Dead End* (1937) and Wellman's *The High and the Mighty* (1954), and an Oscar for her supporting role in John Huston's *Key Largo* (1948).

Merle Oberon *(1911-1979)*, discovered by Korda, given leading British roles in the 1930s, narrowly survived a car-crash during the making of the ill-fated *I, Claudius* (Sternberg, 1937), but was an elfin Cathy in Wyler's *Wuthering Heights* (1939).

Vera-Ellen *(1926-1981)*, dancing partner to Danny Kaye (Humberstone's *Wonder Man*, 1945), Fred Astaire (Walters' *Belle of New York*, 1952), Gene Kelly (Kelly/Donen's *On the Town*, 1949), Donald O'Connor (Walter Lang's *Call Me Madam*, 1953). Retired in 1956.

Ann Sheridan *(1915-1967)* was the Warner 'Oomph Girl' from 1937, wise-cracking in movies alongside Cagney, Bogart and with Reagan in Sam Wood's *King's Row* (1942), but at her best in Hawks' *I was a Male War Bride* (1949) and Sirk's *Take Me to Town* (1953).

Hedy Lamarr *(b.1916)*, scandal perpetually at her heels, had an imperturbable beauty that often outshone her films. They included Fleming's *Tortilla Flat* (1942), Brown's *Come Live With Me* (1941), and De Mille's *Samson and Delilah* (1949).

An instant legend as Scarlett O'Hara in Victor Fleming's *Gone with the Wind* (1939).

With Robert Taylor in LeRoy's *Waterloo Bridge* (1940).

As Emma to Laurence Olivier's Nelson in Korda's *Lady Hamilton* (1941).

Vivien Leigh

(1913-1967)

Half of Hollywood and thousands of would-be Scarletts from all over the States wanted the role that was finally hers in 1938. Chosen as the burning of Atlanta lit up her face, and because her eyes were the same colour as stated in the novel, she fought with her director and co-star, played merry hell with everyone else, and won an Oscar. She had a five-year contract with Korda in the 1930s, played opposite Olivier in William K. Howard's *Fire Over England* (1937), but was almost unknown in the States until *Gone with the Wind* made her an instant legend.

Stardom was a sour affair, the films were few and not as memorable as they might have been (although she was a perfect Queen of the Nile in Pascal's *Caesar and Cleopatra* in 1945), but her bouts of depression and illness left their mark in support to her superlative Blanche Dubois in Elia Kazan's *A Streetcar Named Desire* (1951) and another Oscar was her reward. In unavoidable identification with Scarlett, she seemed fated to self-destruction, almost deserving of it, but her private struggle was with tuberculosis and she was eventually defeated.

In the Korda production of *Anna Karenina* (1948).

With Karl Malden in Kazan's *A Streetcar Named Desire* (1951).

With Warren Beatty in José Quintero's *The Roman Spring of Mrs Stone* (1961).

Ingrid Bergman

(1915-1982)

With Leslie Howard in *Intermezzo* (Ratoff, 1939).

With Bogart in Michael Curtiz's *Casablanca* (1942).

After Swedish films in the 1930s she was brought to Hollywood by Selznick for *Intermezzo*, and would have been stuck with the image of sweet naivety if she hadn't insisted on pursuing darker and more complex roles in *Casablanca* (Curtiz, 1942), *Saratoga Trunk* (Wood, 1945), the Oscar-winning *Gaslight* (Cukor, 1944), and Hitchcock's *Notorious* (1946). Then came the Rossellini affair, the superb *Voyage to Italy* (Rossellini, 1953), and a return to Hollywood acclaim with Litvak's *Anastasia* (1958), for which there was another Oscar. Subsequent successes alternated between stage and screen; she's sadly missed.

With Gary Cooper in *For Whom the Bell Tolls* (Wood, 1943).

With Cooper in *Saratoga Trunk* (Wood, 1945).

With Boyer on the set of Milestone's *Arch of Triumph* (1948).

With Mel Ferrer in Renoir's *Eléna et les Hommes* (1956).

With Charles Boyer and Joseph Cotten in Cukor's *Gaslight* (1944), known in Great Britain as *The Murder in Thornton Square*.

Veronica Lake

(1919-1973)

No respecter of Hollywood, she showed it in her sleepy and contemptuous gaze, conveying a conspiratorial intimacy with the camera that was hard to resist. The curl of hair across the eye became a nationwide fad, attracting such ardent suitors as Onassis and Howard Hughes. Fine in comedy like Preston Sturges' *Sullivan's Travels* (1941) and with Fredric March (whom she loathed) in René Clair's *I Married a Witch* (1942), she was pure dynamite in her trenchcoat films with Alan Ladd (for example, Tuttle's *This Gun for Hire*, 1942), but by 1950 had dropped out of sight, with more scorn than regret for the irredeemable past.

With Joel McCrea in *Sullivan's Travels* (Sturges, 1941).

With Fredric March in *I Married a Witch* (Clair, 1942).

Arletty

(b.1898)

After a music-hall debut in 1918 and many stage appearances, she reached the screen in 1931 with Jean Choux's *Un Chien qui Rapporte*, and continued in movies for some 30 years. Her mocking smile, jaded elegance, and smouldering eyes made her unforgettable as Garance in *Les Enfants du Paradis*, but she was an essential part of innumerable other French classics, including Feyder's *Le Grand Jeu* (1933), Carné's *Le Jour se Lève* (1939), and as the menacing lesbian in Jacqueline Audry's *Huis Clos* (1954).

As the boxer's wife in Marcel Carné's *L'Air de Paris* (1954).

With Louis Jouvet (*left*) in Carné's *Hôtel du Nord* (1938).

With Alain Cuny in Carné's *Les Visiteurs du Soir* (1942).

With Jean-Louis Barrault in Carné's *Les Enfants du Paradis* (1944).

123

Michèle Morgan

(b.1920)

Discovered at 17 by the French director Marc Allégret, she began in his *Gribouille* (1937) and *Orage* (1937), then starred with Gabin in Carné's *Quai des Brumes* (1938). After further successes with Grémillon's *Remorques* (1940) and Feyder's *La Loi du Nord* (1942) she went to Hollywood for Michael Curtiz's *Passage to Marseilles* (1944) and Arthur Ripley's *The Chase* (1946). She made a triumphant return to Europe with Jean Delannoy's *La Symphonie Pastorale* (1946), based on André Gide's novel, which won her the Best Actress Award at Cannes. When her emotions are allowed some range – as in René Clair's *Les Grandes Manoeuvres* (1955) or Cayatte's *Le Miroir a Deux Faces* (1958) – she's a force to be reckoned with, but later films asked little of her except serenity.

With Jean Gabin in Carné's *Quai des Brumes* (1938).

With Bernard Lee in Carol Reed's *Fallen Idol* (1948).

124

With Gérard Philipe in *Les Grandes Manoeuvres* (Clair, 1955).

With Jean Gaven in Jean Delannoy's *Obsession* (1954).

In Yves Allégret's *Les Orgueilleux*, a Venice prizewinner in 1953.

Moira Shearer (b.1926) caught the public imagination for her first screen role as the doomed ballerina in Powell/Pressburger's *The Red Shoes* (1948), and danced through three more films before retiring to family life.

Margaret Lockwood (b.1916) became firmly identified with *The Wicked Lady* (Arliss, 1945), her Gainsborough image already fascinatingly tarnished by the whipping from James Mason in *The Man in Grey* (Arliss. 1943).

Micheline Presle (b.1922) made her screen debut in 1938, starred in Becker's *Falbalas* (1944), and (*left*) with Gérard Philipe in Autant-Lara's *Le Diable au Corps* (1946), A long run of supporting roles followed.

The 1950^s

It was the decade of desperation. As audiences dwindled, the studios tried everything to out-spectacle the television screen – CinemaScope, Cinerama, the 70mm Todd-AO process, and 3-D, which was all the rage for a brief, eye-straining period. Scope films required the minimum amount of technical adjustment to the cinemas, so they were the gimmick that survived. Several directors found the new ratio suited their style perfectly; plenty of actresses, whose best performances often required a horizontal perspective, felt the same way. It was the decade, too, of the glossy 'woman's picture', the rock'n'roll movie, the drive-in horror movie, and the adult movie which dared to speak of subjects too hot for the television stations. Plus a quantity of the now-celebrated worst movies ever made. All these attractions got the teenagers out of the house and on to the streets where they belonged. And the stars continued to twinkle with innocence or smoulder with passion.

Elizabeth Taylor

(b.1932)

At 11 she was a delightful child, appearing among MGM's earliest Technicolor releases with Pal the dog (Lassie), following up with Clarence Brown's masterly *National Velvet* (1944), once intended for Katharine Hepburn. By 1950 she was getting married, on screen in Minnelli's *Father of the Bride* (1950) and for real to the first of a long and confusing line of husbands. Maturing beautifully, she got most of the best non-musical roles around: *A Place in the Sun*, Richard Thorpe's *Ivanhoe* (1952), *Giant*, Edward Dmytryk's

With Burton and Louis Jourdan in *The VIPs* (Asquith, 1963).

With Burton in *Who's Afraid of Virginia Woolf?* (Nichols, 1966).

With Pal in *Lassie Comes Home* (Wilcox, 1943).

With James Dean in *Giant* (Stevens, 1956).

Raintree County (1957), and then, in abrupt contrast, Richard Brooks' *Cat on a Hot Tin Roof* (1958) and the Mankiewicz shocker *Suddenly Last Summer* (1959). The image changed to one of ripe indulgence, punctuated with illness and divorces, but there were two Oscars and plenty more good films.

With Montgomery Clift in *A Place in the Sun* (Stevens, 1951).

With Paul Newman in *Cat on a Hot Tin Roof* (Brooks, 1958).

Queen of all she surveys in Joseph L. Mankiewicz's *Cleopatra* (1963).

Grace Kelly

(1928-1982)

No sooner was she recognized as the most gorgeous new face in world cinema than her career was over and she was a Princess. Her training at the US Academy of Dramatic Art led only to modelling and television commercials before MGM signed her up and loaned her out for an undistinguished debut in Henry Hathaway's *Fourteen Hours* (1951). Pretty but not radiant in *High Noon* and *Mogambo* (Ford, 1953), she got the Hitchcock treatment in 1954 for *Dial M for Murder* and the amazing *Rear Window*, and won an Oscar for George Seaton's *The Country Girl*, in which she rescued husband Bing Crosby from alcoholism. Her last film was the unforgettable *High Society*.

With Ray Milland in Hitchcock's *Dial M for Murder* (1954).

With James Stewart for Hitchcock's *Rear Window* (1954).

With Gary Cooper and (*far left*) Lon Chaney Jr and Thomas Mitchell in Fred Zinnemann's *High Noon* (1952).

With Louis Jourdan in *The Swan* (Vidor, 1956).

With Bing Crosby in *The Country Girl* (Seaton, 1954).

With Bing Crosby in *High Society* (Walters, 1956).

With Cary Grant in Hitchcock's *To Catch a Thief* (1955).

Marilyn Monroe

(1926-1962)

Among her 20 films there are only a few good ones owing little of their quality to her performance but much to her *presence*. That she could act as well as undulate is clear from *The Misfits*, and that she had a fine sense of comedy comes across from *Bus Stop*. She hated symbolism ('I thought symbols were something you clash') and the exaggerated gestures of her songs, walks and dances were achieved as much by parody as in the enthusiasm for her own physique. She strove for more sophisticated talents, as though by marrying Arthur Miller she might become his equal, but she was loved precisely because on screen she was without complications. The popular image was so much at variance with her personal designs that the contradiction, along with the drugs and the inherited instability, finally shook her apart.

In Otto Preminger's *River of No Return* (1954) and (*right*) in *There's No Business Like Show Business* (Lang, 1954).

In Joshua Logan's *Bus Stop* (1956).

With Tony Curtis and Jack Lemmon, in *Some Like It Hot* (Wilder, 1959).

With Clark Gable in *The Misfits* (Huston, 1961).

With Tom Ewell in *The Seven Year Itch* (Wilder, 1955).

Kim Novak

(b.1933)

In 1953 she was 'Miss Deepfreeze', helping to sell refrigerators by leaning on them and her unkindest critics would claim that she never thawed out. Hitchcock's *Vertigo* (1958) may be offered as her best performance, but she goes through it – as required – like a sleepwalker, manipulated and reconstructed according to the passions of others. When, in Aldrich's underrated *Legend of Lylah Clare* (1968), she plays an actress in revolt, the same remoteness comes through: alcoholic hysteria contrives to leave her features serenely unravaged and the ice-cubes unmelted.

With Fred MacMurray in *Pushover* (Quine, 1954).

With Frank Sinatra in *The Man with the Golden Arm* (Preminger, 1956).

134

With William Holden in *Picnic* (Logan, 1955).

With Tyrone Power in *The Eddy Duchin Story* (Sidney, 1956).

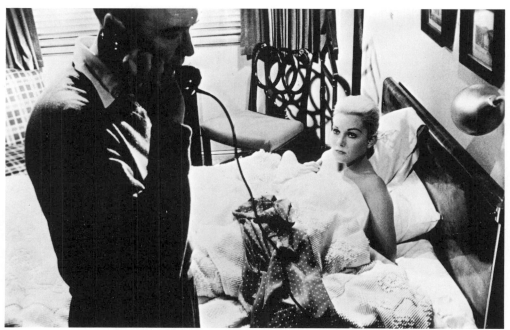

With James Stewart in Hitchcock's *Vertigo* (1958).

As the Broadway actress *Jeanne Eagles* (Sidney, 1957).

With Dean Martin, Ray Walston in Wilder's *Kiss Me Stupid* (1964).

With Humphrey Bogart in *The Barefoot Contessa* (Mankiewicz, 1954).

With Gable in Vincent Sherman's *Lone Star* (1952).

Ava Gardner

(b. 1922)

She has a take-it-or-leave-it look that lets you know any trouble around here would start or end with her. In the 1950s she was exquisitely turned out in the most unexpected places. In Arthur Lewin's roaring romantic melodrama *Pandora and the Flying Dutchman* (1951), truly the kind of fantasy nobody dares make any more, she unleashed the wiles of the world at a glance. As barefoot contessa amid the snows of Kilimanjaro, she was the essence of Hemingway; and the aura of disaster increased around her as she waved Gregory Peck to the end of the world in Kramer's *On the Beach* (1960) and was besieged with Heston at Peking. In *Earthquake* (Robson, 1974) and *City on Fire* (Rakoff, 1979), she continued as ever to remain in the eye of the storm.

With James Mason in *Pandora and the Flying Dutchman* (Lewin, 1951).

With Mel Ferrer, Tyrone Power in *The Sun Also Rises* (King, 1957).

With Heston in Nicholas Ray's *55 Days at Peking* (1963).

In George Cukor's *Bhowani Junction* (1956).

Deborah Kerr

(b.1921)

She was a British export to be proud of, principled, distinguished, uncompromised. Incline as she might towards more torrid activities, the seashore clinch in *From Here to Eternity* evoked not so much shock as sheer disbelief. She was perfect in *The King and I* as the warm-hearted but unyielding governess with a mission to bring enlightenment to the heathen – perfect because, in its musical form, the story requires a comic edge and the true British can be relied upon to laugh at themselves. As with *Tea and Sympathy* (Minnelli, 1956) or Clayton's *The Innocents* (1961), it was inconceivable that scandal or malice could overthrow her. In some exasperation, she finally went back to the stage.

In *Black Narcissus* (Powell/Pressburger, 1947), and (*right*) with Stewart Granger in *King Solomon's Mines* (Marton/Bennett, 1950).

With Burt Lancaster in *From Here to Eternity* (Zinnemann, 1953).

With Yul Brynner in *The King and I* (Lang, 1956).

With David Niven in Delbert Mann's *Separate Tables* (1958).

Maureen O'Hara

(b.1920)

When John Ford admirer Sam Peckinpah made his first film in 1961, the only star he would consider was Maureen O'Hara; *The Deadly Companions* is a tribute to her established screen persona as a woman of fire and sorrow, vengeance and loyalty. Her beauty was wild and startling when she arrived at 19 in Hitchcock's *Jamaica Inn* (1939) and found Charles Laughton's protection in *Hunchback of Notre Dame* (Dieterle, 1939). But after Ford discovered her for *How Green was my Valley*, she matured deliciously through films with Renoir, Borzage, Wellman and Nicholas Ray to become the tempestuous counterpart to John Wayne in four more Ford classics and an ample collection of other movies made the finer by her presence.

With John Wayne in John Ford's *Rio Grande* (1950).

With Walter Pidgeon in *How Green Was My Valley* (Ford, 1941).

With John Wayne in John Ford's *The Quiet Man* (1952).

Patricia Neal

(b.1926)

She was Ronald Reagan's fiancée in her first film, David Butler's *John Loves Mary* (1949), but *The Fountainhead*, with Gary Cooper, showed her to better advantage. After a prize-studded Broadway debut, she was a no-nonsense fighter on screen who could help save the world in *The Day the Earth Stood Still* (Wise, 1951) or defend the truth in Kazan's *Face in the Crowd* (1957). Her Oscar was for *Hud* (Ritt, 1963) since when, heroically recovering from a stroke, she has kept on fighting.

In King Vidor's *The Fountainhead* (1949).

Her Oscar-winning role in Martin Ritt's *Hud* (1963).

Jane Russell

(b.1921)

Despite her warm, up-front smile, Howard Hughes wanted her mean and moody for her first film *The Outlaw* (1943). The publicity was more explosive than the performance but she's restored the balance since then; unlike Monroe, she could be sexy and survive, unflustered by her superstructure. In the 1950s her films could be in snarling mood like Sternberg's *Macao* (1952), but were more often bright and ironic, like *Gentlemen Prefer Blondes* (Hawks, 1953). After relaxing into retirement as a restaurant owner, she's now back in a television soap opera *The Yellow Rose*.

In Lloyd Bacon's *The French Line* (1954).

In Norman Z. McLeod's *The Paleface* (1948).

In Raoul Walsh's *The Tall Men* (1955).

Judy Garland

(1922-1969)

With Margaret O'Brien in *Meet Me in St Louis* (Minnelli, 1944).

At the age of three, baby Frances Gumm was on stage singing 'Jingle Bells', at seven she was in her first movie, and at 14 she had an MGM contract. It all happened too fast for the real girl to keep in touch with the artificial one who, chubby and resourceful on screen, increasingly had to be powered by medicines and drugs. Even at her most legendary, as the Oscar-winning Dorothy in Victor Fleming's *Wizard of Oz* (1939), or in the delectable *Meet Me in St Louis*, she resembled a wax figure on the point of melting – everything about her looked to have been assembled by other hands. But the singing voice, at first raucously holding its own against Mickey Rooney, matured into an instrument that revealed a more authentic Judy Garland, and when it was about all she had left she used it in ruthless desperation to claim a rightful tribute of regret from her audience. The tributes always came, but in the end they were poor comfort for a star on the wrong side of the rainbow.

In Cukor's *A Star is Born* (1954), now restored to full length.

June Allyson

(b.1918)

A self-taught dancer, she was a Broadway chorus-girl and understudy who, when MGM bought *Best Foot Forward* (Buzzell, 1943) went with it to Hollywood and found herself singing 'Treat Me Rough' to Mickey Rooney in *Girl Crazy* (Taurog, 1943). With her husky voice and infectious grin, she was quickly popular although MGM tended to swamp her with other stars in portmanteau musicals like *Till the Clouds Roll By* (Whorf, 1946) and *Words and Music* (Taurog, 1948). Her best movies were *Little Women* (1949) and *The Stratton Story* (Wood, 1949) for which her co-star was James Stewart; he was so impressed that he refused to do *The Glenn Miller Story* and *Strategic Air Command* (Mann, 1955) without her. In the 1960s she had her own television show, and today still makes an occasional reappearance.

With Elizabeth Taylor, Janet Leigh (*left*) and Margaret O'Brien (*right*) in *Little Women* (LeRoy, 1949).

With Walter Pidgeon in *The Secret Heart* (Leonard, 1946).

With James Stewart in *The Glenn Miller Story* (Mann, 1953).

With Alan Ladd in *The McConnell Story* (Douglas, 1955).

Susan Hayward

(1918-1975)

'You'll remember *my* name,' she tells Richard Conte in Mankiewicz's splendid *House of Strangers* (1949), and indeed you could be sure that when Susan Hayward hit the screen there was nowhere else to look. A failed screen test for *Gone with the Wind* was no deterrent – she used it to get a job at Warners. A glowing redhead, she gave each role the intensity of total seriousness, whether courted by John Wayne in the daft epic *The Conqueror* (Powell, 1955) or bronco-busting with Mitchum in *The Lusty Men* (Ray, 1952). Her best portraits were of women who, like herself, tended to get their own way.

In Walter Lang's *With a Song in My Heart* (1952).

With Dana Andrews in Mark Robson's *My Foolish Heart* (1949).

Her Oscar-winning role in *I Want to Live!* (Wise, 1958).

Doris Day

(b. 1924)

She had a faultless voice and a face to match. The fresh, wholesome image came in the 1960s to be associated, in some scorn, with a mythical America of boundless good cheer with hints of naughtiness at lights-out time, but her autobiography reveals a far less contented existence with a succession of unappreciative husbands. They probably felt outclassed by her: she was a dauntingly good comedienne, her choice of songs regularly became hits, and as *Calamity Jane* (Butler, 1953) or in the more thankless role of the agitated average Mum in Hitchcock's *The Man Who Knew Too Much*, she deserved nothing but praise. After the 'glossies' like *Move Over, Darling* (Gordon, 1963), she retired in 1968 to the Doris Day Pet Foundation and the odd margarine commercial.

With Clark Gable in George Seaton's *Teacher's Pet* (1958).

Hoisted aloft in Stanley Donen's *The Pyjama Game* (1957).

With Bernard Miles, Brenda de Banzie, James Stewart and (knifed) Daniel Gelin in Hitchcock's *The Man Who Knew Too Much* (1956); with James Cagney (*left*) and Cameron Mitchell in *Love Me or Leave Me* (Vidor, 1955).

Cyd Charisse

(b.1921)

Nobody has ever had an unkind word to say for her. Whether the taste is for *Singin' in the Rain* (Kelly/Donen, 1952) or for Nicholas Ray's colourful crime masterpiece *Party Girl* (1958), the presence of Cyd Charisse on the screen is enough to bring a general purr of contentment. It's not just the legs, although they're reason enough; from *The Band Wagon* (Minnelli, 1953) to *Silk Stockings* (Mamoulian, 1957), she contrived to be effortlessly elegant and perfectly co-ordinated. She gave it all up in the 1960s and many a heart has never mended since.

Parked beside some eggs in a lunatic promotional photo.

Modelling for fashion in 1952.

147

Lauren Bacall

(b.1924)

The hooded eyes and the deep, sultry voice were made for *films noirs*, the cinema of the underworld. Like a David Goodis heroine, she's been around, seen it all, and has no illusions left. Actually she was only 19 and a model for *Harper's Bazaar* when Hawks surrounded her with Hemingway and Hoagy Carmichael for *To Have and Have Not* (1944), in partnership with Bogart whom she promptly married. They could match each other growl for growl, audiences loved them, and the next stop was Chandler territory in *The Big Sleep*, followed by the Goodis story *Dark Passage* in 1947, and Huston's *Key Largo* (1948). Later she proved that 'the look' worked just as well for comedy in *How to Marry a Millionaire* and Minnelli's *Designing Woman* (1957). And it works well on stage, too, as a 1970 Tony Award confirmed.

With Bogart in Howard Hawks' *The Big Sleep* (1946).

With Bogart in Delmer Daves' *Dark Passage* (1947).

With Marilyn Monroe in *How to Marry a Millionaire* (Negulesco, 1953).

Jean Simmons

(b.1925)

She picked her films with care, and improved them by taking part – even in the early Gainsborough musical days and in *Way to the Stars* (Asquith, 1945). A Rank starlet, she was Estella in David Lean's *Great Expectations* (1946), a jewel of an Indian girl in the Powell/Pressburger *Black Narcissus* (1947), and a mesmerising Ophelia to Olivier's Hamlet. Possibly at her peak in 1960 with *Elmer Gantry* (Brooks) and *Spartacus* (Kubrick), she gradually gave up films for television and the stage.

With Gregory Peck in William Wyler's *The Big Country* (1958).

With Richard Burton in *The Robe* (Koster, 1953).

As Ophelia in Olivier's *Hamlet* (1948).

With Marlon Brando, Frank Sinatra, Vivien Blaine in *Guys and Dolls* (Mankiewicz, 1955).

149

Debbie Reynolds (b.1932), ex-majorette and teenage 'Miss Burbank', destined to become Carrie Fisher's mother, was sweetness and light in the 1950s for *Singin' in the Rain* and *The Tender Trap* (Walters, 1955) but rather too syrupy as *The Unsinkable Molly Brown* (Walters, 1964) and *The Singing Nun* (Koster, 1965), and today produces keep-fit videos.

Janet Leigh (b.1927); inescapably linked with motel showers (Hitchcock's *Psycho*, 1960) and killer rabbits (Claxton's *Night of the Lepus*, 1972), her luscious and intelligent performances in musicals, epics and Westerns of the 1950s deserve better memory. She was super in *Scaramouche* (Sidney, 1952), thrilling in *Touch of Evil* (Welles, 1957).

Kathryn Grayson (b.1922), with her impermeable features, partnered Howard Keel note for decibel in such stand-and-deliver musicals as *Show Boat* (Sidney, 1951) and *Kiss Me Kate* (Sidney, 1953), and was ideal for Romberg in *The Desert Song* (Humberstone, 1953) and for Oreste in *The Vagabond King* (Curtiz, 1956). She still makes the musical rounds on stage.

Mitzi Gaynor (b.1931), best known for washing men out of her hair (Logan's *South Pacific*, 1958), was a vivacious and prolific dancer on the 1950s screen after a stage start at the age of four. A bundle of energy in movies like *There's No Business Like Show Business* (Lang, 1954), Cukor's *Les Girls* (1957), or Gordon's *For Love or Money* (1963), she now does the nightclub circuit and some television.

Leslie Caron (b.1931); her movie career began right at the top with Minnelli's *An American in Paris* (1951), where her waif-like charm and her expertise as a top Parisian ballet-dancer made a huge impact. With Fred Astaire in *Daddy Long Legs* (Negulesco, 1955) *right*, (*above*) as *Lili* (Walters, 1953), *Gaby* (Bernhardt, 1956), *Gigi* (Minnelli, 1958) and *Fanny* (Logan, 1961) she was an enduring delight; today, she's still applying grace and versatility to international movies.

Pier Angeli (1932-1971), once James Dean's girl and like him destined for tragedy, her fragile freshness somehow never had much chance. Irresistible as Zinnemann's *Teresa* (1951) and in Richard Brooks' *The Light Touch* (1951), she was wasted in *The Silver Chalice* (Saville, 1955) and *Merry Andrew* (Kidd, 1958), but excellent alongside Paul Newman (*above*) in Robert Wise's *Somebody Up There Likes Me* (1956) and in Guy Green's *The Angry Silence* (1960).

Rhonda Fleming (b.1923) had the kind of looks that were at their best in Technicolor, seemed destined for pirate films and Westerns, but appeared to advantage in unexpected places like *Out of the Past* (Tourneur, 1947), *Cry Danger* (Parrish, 1951), and *While the City Sleeps* (Lang, 1956).

Shelley Winters (b.1922) victim in thrillers like *Johnny Stool Pigeon* (Castle, 1949) – with Dan Duryea (*above*) – and *A Double Life* (Cukor, 1948). Later she brought a distracted splendour to Kubrick's *Lolita* (1962) and Corman's *Bloody Mama* (1970).

Julie Harris (b.1925) went from Broadway to movies as stormy teenager in *Member of the Wedding* (Zinnemann, 1952), and had winners with *I am a Camera* (Cornelius, 1955) and Kazan's *East of Eden* (1955) with Raymond Massey, James Dean (*above*).

Jeanne Crain *(b.1925)* won Oscar nomination for Kazan's *Pinky* (1949) but became better known for well-groomed showings in 1950s dramas like *Duel in the Jungle* (Marshall, 1954) and *The Second Greatest Sex* (Marshall, 1955).

Donna Reed *(b.1921)* confirmed for all of us and James Stewart that *It's a Wonderful Life* (Capra, 1946), won her supporting actress Oscar for *From Here to Eternity* (Zinnemann, 1953). She had her own television show from 1958 to 1966.

Ruth Roman *(b.1923)* went from serial Jungle Queen to Hitchcock's *Strangers on a Train* (1951) and Fregonese's *Blowing Wild* (1953) with Gary Cooper, later taking up television with *Dr Kildare* and others.

Eleanor Parker *(b.1922)* won Oscar nomination for *Caged* (Cromwell, 1950), had a decade of goodies like *Detective Story* (Wyler, 1951) and *Man with the Golden Arm* (Preminger, 1956) before returning to supporting roles.

Jane Powell *(b.1929)*; after her own radio programme at 11, she sang her way through MGM musicals from *Holiday in Mexico* (Sidney, 1946) to *Hit the Deck* (Rowland, 1955). Best of the lot was Donen's *Seven Brides for Seven Brothers* (1954), pictured above (with Russ Tamblyn in mid-air). Just as vivacious in Leisen's *The Girl Most Likely* (1958), she gave up the screen for Broadway successes continuing into the 1970s.

Silvana Mangano

(b. 1930)

Given her statuesque appearance in later films, it's easy to forget that she came to general notice by standing up to her thighs in the rice-fields, a stormy and earthily assertive peasant-girl in *Bitter Rice* (De Santis, 1948). Dancer, model, then winner of the 'Miss Rome' contest, she boogied from the rice fields into marriage to Dino de Laurentiis, who generously allowed her to continue as a neo-realist sex-bomb in the 1950s, and then to look quite disturbing in costumed co-productions like Fleischer's *Barabbas* (1962). The classics closed in with Pasolini's *Oedipus Rex* (1967) and *Medea* (1970), and by the time of *Death in Venice* (Visconti, 1971) she had acquired a mask-like and almost melancholic calm.

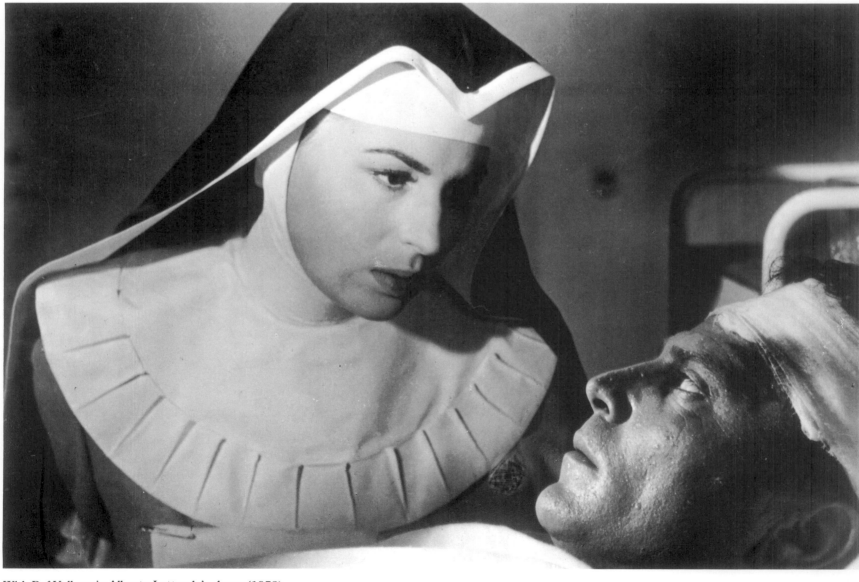

With Raf Vallone in Alberto Lattuada's *Anna* (1952).

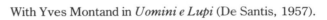

In Pasolini's *Teorema* (1968).

With Yves Montand in *Uomini e Lupi* (De Santis, 1957).

With Amedo Nazzari in *Il Lupo della Sila* (Coletti, 1949).

With Jeffrey Horn in Lattuada's *La Tempesta* (1958).

Gina Lollobrigida

(b. 1927)

More of a storm warning than an actress, she had no compunction about using her resonant curves to capture worldwide attention and by the 1950s was nicely in control of a Hollywood career. Beginning as a model in the *fumetti* comics, she made her first film in 1946, Costa's *Elisir d'Amore*, and was soon working for top European directors – Christian-Jaque, Alessandro Blasetti, René Clair, and Mario Soldati. After being picked to star with Humphrey Bogart in Huston's *Beat the Devil* (1953) and with De Sica for two *Bread, Love and...* comedies directed by Comencini in 1954 and widely shown in the States, she was an established attraction. Looking good in any style, she was in Carol Reed's *Trapeze* (1956) and King Vidor's memorable *Solomon and Sheba* (1959). When by the late 1960s she got fed up with the same old routines, she turned to photography and documentaries.

With Gérard Philipe in Christian-Jaque's *Fanfan la Tulipe*. (1952).

In Luigi Zampa's *La Romana* (1954).

In René Clair's *Les Belles de Nuit* (1952).

With Pierre Brasseur in Dassin's *Where the Hot Wind Blows* (1959).

In *Beautiful but Dangerous* (Leonard, 1955).

With Anthony Quinn in Delannoy's *Notre Dame de Paris* (1956).

Anna Magnani

(1908-1973)

Laughing or crying or both at once, there were no half measures for Magnani. In the Italian musichall she was phenomenal; some of the impact comes through in De Sica's *Teresa Venerdì* (1941) where, capped with white plumes, she appears as a show girl. Transferred to the screen, the joy or fury had a massive desperation; her death in Rossellini's *Roma, Città Aperta* (1945) seemed to summarize the wartime tragedies of Italy, while her portrait in Visconti's *Bellissima* (1951) was the *cri de coeur* of every ambitious parent. She won an Oscar for *The Rose Tattoo* (written for her by Tennessee Williams), worked with Brando for *The Fugitive Kind* (Lumet, 1960), but came home tumultuously for Pasolini's *Mamma Roma* (1962), and her heart stayed put.

In Rossellini's *Roma, Città Aperta* (1945).

In Daniel Mann's *The Rose Tattoo* (1955).

With Joseph Cotten in *The Third Man* (Reed, 1949).

With Farley Granger in Visconti's *Senso* (1954).

Alida Valli

(b.1921)

A popular comedienne between 1936 and 1945, from the age of 19 she was also in films, notably Soldati's *Piccolo Mondo Antico* (1940). Then Selznick saw her as another Ingrid Bergman and she went to Hollywood for Hitchcock's *The Paradine Case* (1947) and Carol Reed's *The Third Man* (1949). Pichel's ham-fisted *Miracle of the Bells* (1949) seemed a good reason to return to Europe, and Visconti's *Senso* (1954), an operatic tale of passion and betrayal, confirmed it was a wise decision. Her haunting presence has been the guarantee of quality in many subsequent films, by Colpi, Torre Nilsson, Bertolucci, and by Eduardo de Gregorio for a remake of Henry James' *The Aspern Papers* in 1982.

With Georges Wilson in Colpi's *Une Aussi Longue Absence* (1961).

Simone Signoret

(b.1921)

Solid and accusing, she always
seems to be concealing a limitless
capacity for pain under an
impassive exterior. In the films by
her first husband, Yves Allégret,
Dédée d'Anvers (1948) and
Manèges (1950), and in Maurice
Tourneur's *Impasse des Anges*
(1948), she was warm and intense
but already wistful. As the
prostitute in Ophüls' *La Ronde*
(1950), as Carné's *Thérèse Raquin*
(1953), and then as the ruthless
schoolteacher in Clouzot's *Les
Diaboliques* (1955), her image of
resigned menace and
determination grew to be a habit.
It won her an Oscar for *Room at
the Top*, was ideal for Melville's
L'Armée des Ombres (1969), and
remains an imposing and magnetic
screen presence.

With Raf Vallone in Marcel Carné's *Thérèse Raquin* (1953).

With Mylène Demongeot in *Les Sorcières de Salem* (Rouleau, 1957).

In Henri-Georges Clouzot's *Les Diaboliques* (1955).

With Laurence Harvey in Jack Clayton's *Room at the Top* (1959).

Anouk Aimée

(b. 1932)

After dancing lessons at the Opera of Marseilles and drama classes in Paris, she was chosen at 15 by Carné to appear in *La Fleur de l'Age* (1947); it was unfinished but she went on to make *La Maison Sous la Mer* (Calef, 1947) and *Les Amants de Vérone* (Cayatte/Prévert, 1949). From the start, she had an aura of languid fragility that fired the imagination of romantic directors like Alexandre Astruc, who used her as an icon of the unattainable in his short film *Le Rideau Craimoisi* (1953), and made her the ideal star for Becker, Cukor, Demy, and Lelouch. Always transient and uncommitted, her private world an unmeasurable distance away, she was perfect as Demy's *Lola* (1961) and Cukor's *Justine* (1969), and as the lonely, gently dying mother in *Mon Premier Amour* (Chouraqui, 1978).

With Yul Brynner in Litvak's *The Journey* (1959).

With Claude Rains in *The Man who Watched Trains Go By* (French, 1952).

With Marcello Mastroianni in Fellini's *Otto e Mezzo* (1963).

With Jean-Louis Trintignant in Lelouch's *Un Homme et Une Femme* (1966).

With Gérard Philipe in Becker's *Montparnasse '19* (1958).

With John Vernon in George Cukor's *Justine* (1969).

Françoise Arnoul

(b.1931)

One of the many reasons for celebrating Renoir's marvellous *French Can-Can* (1955) is Françoise Arnoul's performance as the cabaret girl in love with the boss (Jean Gabin), learning the hard way that business comes first. Born in Algeria, she went to Paris as a teenager determined to get into movies, and began with Willy Rozier's *L'Epave* (1949). Popular with all the French directors, she was everywhere in the 1950s, although it was Vadim's *Sait-On Jamais* (1956) which got her into the sex-kitten roles when Bardot wasn't available. Pretty and provocative in Pierre Kast's *La Morte-Saison des Amours* (1961) and Costa-Gavras' *Sleeping-Car Murders* (1965), she doesn't get banned these days (as happened with a couple of the 1950s shockers) but remains good to watch, as in Jacques Ruffio's *Violette et François* (1977).

In Renoir's *French Can-Can* (1955).

With Gabin in *Des Gens Sans Importance* (Verneuil, 1955).

Marina Vlady

(b. 1938)

With Claude Thierry in Cayatte's *Avant le Déluge* (1954).

With Claude Laydu in Pellegrini's *Sinfonia d'Amore* (1955).

With Serge Reggiani in Robert Hossein's *Les Salauds Vont en Enfer* (1955).

Inscrutably poised as the Parisian housewife earning her keep by prostitution in Godard's *Deux ou Trois Choses que Je Sais d'Elle* (1967), she entered a welcome new phase in a career dating back to a screen debut at 11. A pneumatic adolescent, she married actor-director Robert Hossein in 1955 and played hell-raising swim-suited roles, filling out dramatically as she went along. Winning the Best Actress Award at Cannes in 1963 as the insatiable wife who kills off her husband in Ferreri's *L'Ape Regina*, she became an international star of considerable range, working in Hungary, Italy, Russia, and Finland for Jasný's *The Suicide* (1984).

Brigitte Bardot

(b. 1934)

She became the world's foremost sex symbol in 1956, when in France she was more talked about than politics. She had been transformed by her husband Roger Vadim from the timid, awkward daughter of a wealthy, strait-laced family ('I was ugly, with thin hair, spectacles, and braces on my teeth') to the controversial 'new woman' of the rock'n'roll era, wild, sensual, and reason enough to send one or two luckless cinema managers to jail in the States for showing *And God Created Woman* (Vadim, 1956). By 1960 she was a millionairess and suicidal, her story told with sympathy and style by Louis Malle in *La Vie Privée* (1962), and movies were made only if she felt like doing them, such as *Viva Maria!* (Malle, 1965) or *Shalako* (1968). Her best, Godard's *Le Mépris* (1963), took years to surface, and by 1973 she had retired, horrified by her image, to devote herself to protecting wildlife.

With Roger Pigaut in *La Lumière d'en Face* (Lacomb, 1955).   With Gabin in Duvivier's *La Femme et le Pantin* (1958).

In Michel Boisrond's *Une Parisienne* (1957).

In Henri-Georges Clouzot's *La Vérité* (1960).

With Sean Connery in *Shalako* (Dmytryk, 1968).

Mylène Demongeot

(b. 1938)

When the Bardot style was all the rage she was an ideal stand-in, adding humour and passion to the sex-kitten role. Her first film was Leonide Moguy's *Les Enfants de l'Amour* (1953), but it was as Yves Montand's wide-eyed mistress in *Les Sorcières de Salem* (Rouleau, 1957), a version of Arthur Miller's *The Crucible* that won a collective prize for its cast, that she attracted international projects. There were films in the States (*Bonjour Tristesse*, 1958) and in Britain (Ralph Thomas' *Upstairs and Downstairs*, 1959), and plenty in Europe – although little of lasting merit. Happily married to Marc Simenon, son of the novelist Georges, she still makes the occasional movie.

With Alain Delon in *Faibles Femmes* (Boisrond, 1958).

With Jean Seberg, David Niven in *Bonjour Tristesse* (Preminger, 1957).

With Peter Baldwin in *Un Amore a Roma* (Risi, 1961).

Maria Schell

(b. 1926)

With joyful smile and supplicant eyebrows, she brought a natural warmth and pathos to her roles, usually as the loyal mistress only too likely to be discarded. An Austrian, she began her film career in a Swiss production, *Steinbruch* (Steiner, 1944), but it was ten years until, with a Best Actress Award at Cannes for *Die Letzte Brücke*, she began getting top-quality work in Europe (with Clément, Astruc and Visconti) and then in the States. She starred with Yul Brynner in Brooks' *The Brothers Karamazov* (1958), in Delmer Daves' *The Hanging Tree* (1959), and in Anthony Mann's *Cimarron* (1960) with Glenn Ford. Pausing to raise a family in the 1960s, she returned for intermittent film and television performances, and was to be seen in Richard Donner's *Superman: the Movie* (1978).

With Bernhard Wicki in *Die Letzte Brücke* (Kautner, 1953).

In René Clément's *Gervaise* (1956), based on Zola.

With Mastroianni in Visconti's *Le Notti Bianche* (1957).

With Christian Marquand in Astruc's *Une Vie* (1958).

169

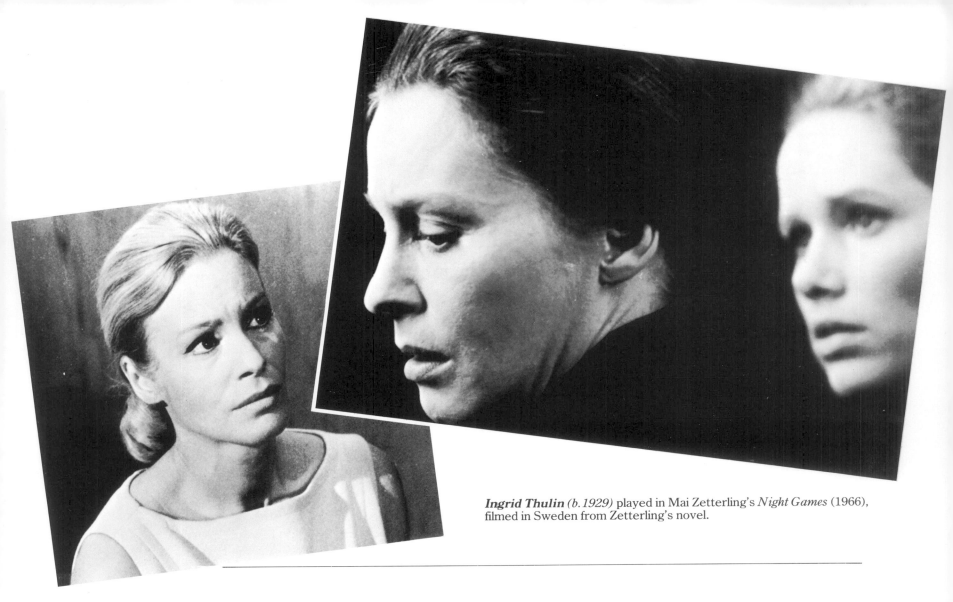

Ingrid Thulin (b. 1929) played in Mai Zetterling's *Night Games* (1966), filmed in Sweden from Zetterling's novel.

Among the many fine actresses brought to the screen by the Swedish director Ingmar Bergman, three were internationally launched by his films in the 1950s. **Ingrid Thulin** had made several films before his *Wild Strawberries* (1957), went to Hollywood in 1961 for Minnelli's remake of *Four Horsemen of the Apocalypse* and returned to Europe for *The Silence* (Bergman, 1963), *La Guerre est Finie* (Resnais, 1966) and Visconti's *The Damned* (1969). **Harriet Andersson** matured from *Summer with Monika* (1953) to a startling performance in the Oscar-winning *Through a Glass Darkly* (1961), won the Best Actress Award at Cannes for husband Jörn Donner's *To Love* (1964), starred in Sidney Lumet's *The Deadly Affair* (1966), and was in top form for *Cries and Whispers* (Bergman, 1972). **Bibi Andersson** won a Best Actress Award at Cannes with *So Close to Life* (1958), and was an impressive presence in Sjöman's *The Mistress* (1962), Bergman's *Persona* (1966), *The Kremlin Letter* (Huston, 1970), and *Quintet* (Altman, 1979).

Harriet Andersson (b. 1932) in *Adventure Starts Here* (Donner, 1965).

Bibi Andersson *(b. 1935)*, with Bergman (*left*) and actor-director Victor Sjöström during the filming of *Wild Strawberries* (1957).

Hildegarde Knef *(b. 1925)* was in some of the first post-war German films, notably Wolfgang Staudte's *The Murderers are Amongst Us* (1946), and was a success both in Europe with Carol Reed's *The Man Between* (1953), Noel Langley's *Svengali* (1954) – pictured here – and Claude Chabrol's *Landru* (1962), and in the States with Billy Wilder's *Fedora* (1978).

Giulietta Masina *(b.1920)* made her debut in Rossellini's *Paisa* (1946) but became widely known for her spirited, clownish performances in films by her husband Fellini – classics like *La Strada* (1954), *Il Bidone* (1955), and in 1957 *Le Notti di Cabiria* (*above right*) in which, despite brutal treatment, she gamely continued to look for happiness. In Fellini's *Giulietta degli Spiriti* (1965) she was no longer ragged but the search continued.

Rossana Podestà *(b.1934)* had an epic figure for the 1950s, made the most of the new Hercules and Pompeii craze, and put out a boat or two as Robert Wise's *Helen of Troy* (1955).

Bernadette Lafont *(b.1938)* came triumphantly in with the New Wave, and from Truffaut's *Les Mistons* (1957) and Chabrol's *Le Beau Serge* (1958) – *above* – was the pouting, fearless sex-queen of the new best-sellers. Producing curves where others didn't even have body, she grew into an accomplished comedienne.

Jacqueline Sassard (b.1940); her placidly challenging air was first filmed by Lattuada in *Guendalina* (1957) *right*, with Raf Mattioli, but it was as the dangerously desirable student in Losey's *Accident* (1967) *above*, with Dirk Bogarde, that she really registered, along with her intriguing role in Chabrol's *Les Biches* (1968).

Pascale Petit (b.1938), seemed to get a useful share of the good-girl-gone-bad roles in such exploitation films as Carné's 'beat generation' *Les Tricheurs* (1958), Bolognini's *La Notte Brava* (1959).

Dany Carrel (b.1935); born in Vietnam, began her screen career in 1953, and was habitually the perky, scheming brunette in films like Julien Duvivier's *Pot-Bouille* (1957) *above*, with Gérard Philipe.

173

Sylva Koscina (b.1934), came to Rome from Yugoslavia, failed a screen test and got into movies by sheer looks and determination, with (above) Pietro Germi's *Il Ferrovière* (1956) which led to copious international productions.

Virginia McKenna (b.1931) was the embodiment of British courage in the 1950s with films like *The Cruel Sea* (Frend, 1953), *A Town Like Alice* (Lee, 1956) *above*, and *Carve Her Name with Pride* (Gilbert, 1958); later alternating between wildlife and the stage, she deserves to be seen more in the cinema.

Martine Carol (1922-1967) was the most daring star of French cinema in the early 1950s, much given to bubble-baths and casual undress before Bardot arrived to raise the temperature; often directed by husband Christian-Jaque (as here, with Charles Boyer, for *Nana*, 1955), she was in at least one undisputed masterpiece as Max Ophüls' *Lola Montès* (1955).

the 1960s

In the French 'New Wave' at the end of the 1950s, young directors suddenly arrived to create cheap, rough movies that caused, briefly, quite a stir. With them, a new breed of performers was launched, casual, clever, and light on their feet. Hollywood retaliated with customary daring, and released the new *Ben Hur*, the new *Cleopatra*, the new *Mutiny on the Bounty*. Such blockbusting originals were often, ironically, made in European studios, with local talents and facilities, to keep the costs down. And often they were sold to television after just three years to keep the revenues up. So for any actress prepared to travel, prospects of gainful employment were excellent, with the bonus that thanks to television she might even become a household name overnight. And although the ubiquitous New Wave style, quickly filched by the Warhol and Underground film factories, tended to expose all for the sake of a dubious stardom, this was also, fortunately, the era of Mary Poppins.

Audrey Hepburn

(b.1929)

Her childhood in Holland was one of contrasts; daughter of a Dutch Baroness, she was training for the ballet amid servants and private tutors when the Nazis invaded and she and her family became involved in the Resistance. A frail teenager, she only narrowly survived the war, resuming her dancing career in 1948 in London at the Ballet Rambert and appearing in revues like *High Button Shoes* and *Sauce Tartare*. There had been a tiny role as an air stewardess in a Dutch film *Nederland in 7 Lessen* (1948), she was accepted by Associated British for bit-parts in films like *The Lavender Hill Mob* (Crichton, 1951), but in no time she was

As the princess in William Wyler's *Roman Holiday* (1953).

With Maurice Chevalier in Wilder's *Love in the Afternoon* (1957).

As Eliza in George Cukor's *My Fair Lady* (1964).

With Mel Ferrer in King Vidor's *War and Peace* (1956).

recruited to play *Gigi* on Broadway, and Wyler's *Roman Holiday* (1953), with Gregory Peck and an Oscar, launched her into a spectacular series of romantic comedies in the 1950s.

With her demure, balletic grace, her crisp, fragile diction, and the winning combination of aristocratic assurance and impulsive insecurity, she was sheer delight in films like Wilder's *Sabrina* (1954), Donen's *Funny Face* (1957), and as Natasha in King Vidor's superb *War and Peace* (1956). For her husband Mel Ferrer she made *Green Mansions* in 1959, and the casting as W.H. Hudson's 'nature girl' seemed perfect, but she was more authentic as Maurice Chevalier's daughter in Wilder's *Love in the Afternoon*. The magic was just as strong in Cukor's *My Fair Lady* (1964), although in controversial dramas like Wyler's *The Children's Hour* (1961), Huston's *The Unforgiven* (1960), and Terence Young's chilling *Wait Until Dark* (1967) she was clearly capable of more complicated characterizations. Too little seen today, she emerges for occasional pleasant surprises like Lester's *Robin and Marian* (1976).

With Peter Finch in Fred Zinnemann's *The Nun's Story* (1959).

With Cary Grant in Stanley Donen's *Charade* (1963).

As the trapped blind girl in *Wait Until Dark* (Young, 1967).

177

Shirley MacLaine

(b. 1934)

For Shirley, the Best Actress Oscar for her role as the chaotic, charismatic Aurora in James L. Brooks' *Terms of Endearment* (1983) was long overdue. In 26 years of movies, there had been four other Oscar nominations and some near misses, but there was no mistaking this one. In a part that allowed the MacLaine talent its full uninhibited range, she was waif-like, tough, eccentric, sly, scatterbrained and sexy, in reminder of previous incarnations as varied as the barmaid in *Some Came Running*, the floozie in Wilder's *Irma la Douce* (1963), the hoofer in Fosse's *Sweet Charity* (1969), the Western pal to Glenn Ford in *The Sheepman* (Marshall, 1958), the Eastern pal to Yves Montand in *My Geisha* (Cardiff, 1961), and the lift-girl in Wilder's *The Apartment.* Today much given to one-woman shows and mildly scandalous memoirs, she's on equal terms with all the endearment around.

With (*from left*) John Forsythe, Mildred Natwick, Edmund Gwenn in Hitchcock's *The Trouble with Harry* (1956).

With Frank Sinatra, Maurice Chevalier in Walter Lang's *Can-Can* (1960).

With Frank Sinatra, Dean Martin in Minnelli's *Some Came Running* (1958).

With Robert Newton, Cantinflas, David Niven in Michael Anderson's *Around the World in 80 Days* (1956).

With Jack Lemmon in Billy Wilder's *The Apartment* (1960).

Julie Andrews

(b.1935)

The role of Mary Poppins, first considered for Bette Davis, was urged on Julie Andrews by Walt Disney after he had seen her in *Camelot* on Broadway in 1961. Doubtful about starting her screen life as a flying nanny, she was more interested in filming her stage hit *My Fair Lady*, but when she lost out to Audrey Hepburn, Julie got her revenge with Oscars for both *Mary Poppins* and, the following year, *The Sound of*

Music. The Andrews image broadened immediately, however, with Hitchcock's *Torn Curtain* (1966), and while singing and dancing remained in the repertoire for *Thoroughly Modern Millie* (Hill, 1967) and *Star!* (Wise, 1968), the slightly reproving charm has given way to a more ironic presence in marital comedies by husband director Blake Edwards like '*10*' (1979) and *S.O.B.* (1981).

As Maria in Robert Wise's *The Sound of Music* (1965).

With Karen Dotrice, Matthew Garber, Dick Van Dyke in Robert Stevenson's *Mary Poppins* (1964).

Anne Bancroft

(b. 1931)

After starting in *Don't Bother to Knock* (Baker, 1952), she freelanced on stage and television until the film of her Broadway hit *The Miracle Worker* won her an Oscar. For a while she seemed typecast in roles requiring toughness and sacrifice, as in Clayton's *The Pumpkin Eater* and John Ford's *Seven Women* (1965). But comedy began to break through with *The Graduate* (Nichols, 1967), and the two films with husband Mel Brooks, *Silent Movie* (1976) and *To Be Or Not To Be* (1983), have confirmed her remarkable range.

With Patty Duke in Arthur Penn's *The Miracle Worker* (1962).

Wife and mother on the point of breakdown in *The Pumpkin Eater* (Clayton, 1964).

With Shirley MacLaine in Herbert Ross's *The Turning Point* (1977).

Ann-Margret

(b.1941)

Her striking appearance and explosive dancing meant that she was more an object for contemplation than an actress in the 1960s. Formerly a jazz singer and comedy foil to George Burns and Jack Benny, she arrived on the screen in Capra's *Pocketful of Miracles* (1961) and really hit her stride with *Bye, Bye Birdie* (Sidney, 1963). Then *Carnal Knowledge* (1971) indicated a change of pace, and with her low-key performances in Alan Bridges' *Return of the Soldier* (1983) and as the mother with ten kids and only a year to live in the prizewinning television weepie *Who Will Love My Children?* (Erman, 1983), she has reached an impressive new stage in her career to parallel continuing cabaret work.

With Alain Delon in Ralph Nelson's *Once a Thief* (1965).

With Jack Nicholson in Mike Nichols' *Carnal Knowledge* (1971).

With Elvis Presley in *Love in Las Vegas* (Sidney, 1963).

In José Ferrer's remake of the musical *State Fair* (1962).

Natalie Wood

(1938-1981)

She was in movies at the age of five, and devoted the rest of her life to them, always photogenic, always a major star, even if the films themselves were often largely expendable. After a huge hit at nine in *Miracle on 34th Street* (1947), a Capra-esque comedy about a little girl who believes she has met Santa Claus, she was captivating in *Rebel Without a Cause* (1955), becoming for a while a part of the awesome James Dean legend. The role of the troubled but basically good-hearted teenager was one that her fresh and ingenuous looks were able to maintain for another ten years, although strong-willed independence was also part of the image.

She was the lost girl well worth recovering from the Indians in John Ford's masterpiece *The Searchers* (1956), or from psychopath Raymond Burr in Frank Tuttle's *Cry in the Night* (1956). She was Gene Kelly's starstruck discovery in *Marjorie Morningstar* (Rapper, 1958), and a Kansas Juliet to newcomer Warren Beatty's Romeo for William Inge's tale of precarious passion in *Splendour in the Grass* (1961), for which she won an Oscar nomination. It was then but a step to *West Side Story* (1961) in which, a Puerto Rican Juliet this time, her joy and her sorrow were enough to melt many a heart beyond repair.

Humour and sex-appeal combined for LeRoy's *Gypsy* (1962) and for two Robert Mulligan films, *Love with the Proper Stranger* (1963) and *Inside Daisy Clover* (1965). She was a deliriously sensual swinger in Mazursky's *Bob & Carol & Ted & Alice* (1969) before retreating from the cinema for a while in the 1970s. The regrettable *Meteor* (Neame, 1979) revealed a new, rather grimmer Natalie, and with Trumbull's *Brainstorm* (begun in 1981, released in 1983) a fresh start seemed imminent. Tragically, it was not to be.

With John Payne in George Seaton's *Miracle on 34th Street* (1947).

With Sal Mineo, James Dean in Nicholas Ray's *Rebel Without a Cause* (1955).

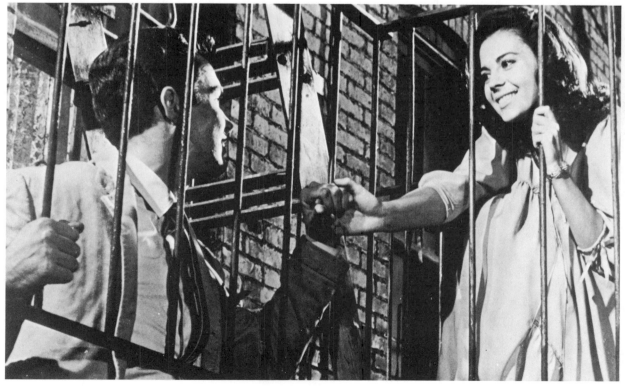

With Richard Beymer in Robert Wise's *West Side Story* (1961).

183

As if being married to Paul Newman were not enough, **Joanne Woodward** has been one of the most prolific and impressive screen actresses. Moving from television to cinema in 1955, she won an Oscar for *The Three Faces of Eve* (Johnson, 1957), and continued to impress with *The Fugitive Kind* (Lumet, 1960), and four films by her husband: *Rachel, Rachel* (1968), *The Effect of Gamma Rays on Man-in-the-Moon Marigolds* (1972), *The Shadow Box* (1980), and *Harry and Son* (1983).

Something of a cult has grown up around **Tuesday Weld**. A teenager with a wicked reputation in the 1950s, she was in *Rock, Rock, Rock* (Price, 1956) at 13, appeared in a slew of nonsense movies, and was suddenly very interesting indeed in Jewison's *The Cincinnati Kid* (1965), the weird thriller *Pretty Poison* (1968), and Henry Jaglom's equally weird *A Safe Place* (1971). She's still around, but not enough, in Leone's *Once Upon a Time in America* (1984).

Joanne Woodward *(b.1930)*

Tuesday Weld *(b.1943)* with Anthony Perkins in Noel Black's *Pretty Poison* (1968).

Jean Seberg *(1938-1979)* had one of the saddest lives in cinema history after her crew-cut debut as Preminger's *Saint Joan* (1957). A dislocated career swung between Godard's *A Bout de Souffle* in 1960 (*above*, with Jean-Paul Belmondo), Rossen's *Lilith* (1964) and Logan's *Paint Your Wagon* (1969). There were four marriages, much political scandal, and a series of breakdowns.

Eva Marie Saint *(b.1924)*, despite Hitchcock's success in making her smoulder for *North by Northwest* (1959), never seemed to muster quite enough passion after her Oscar-winning debut in Kazan's *On the Waterfront* (1954), but still looks cool on television.

Anita Ekberg *(b.1931)*, former Miss Universe contestant, graciously endured some Hollywood glamour-girl roles before making a splash with Fellini's *La Dolce Vita* (1969), and continues to put up a bold front in some occasional hokum.

Mia Farrow (b.1945) went from a drama competition to Broadway to two years of television's *Peyton Place* to marriage with Frank Sinatra to stardom in 1968 with Polanski's *Rosemary's Baby* and Losey's *Secret Ceremony*. Her look of stark terror gradually sobered via marriage to André Previn into tremulous disquiet for Clayton's *The Great Gatsby* (1974) *above* with Robert Redford, and Altman's *A Wedding* (1978).

Capucine (b.1935) was a top fashion model cast as a Russian princess in *Song Without End* (Vidor/Cukor, 1960); once she learned English, she drifted with elegant unconcern through a couple of Peter Sellers comedies, Fellini's *Satyricon* (1969), and Young's *Red Sun* (1971).

Lee Remick (b.1935), reliable keen-eyed lady, formerly spelling trouble in Preminger's *Anatomy of a Murder* (1959) – pictured here with James Stewart – now more restrained in *Telefon* (Siegel, 1977) and *The Europeans* (Ivory, 1979).

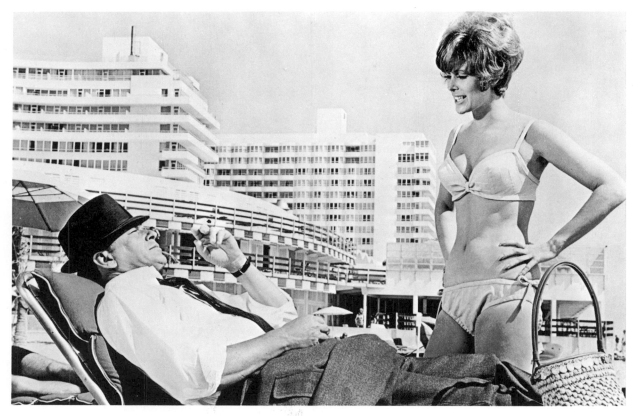

Jill St John (b.1940), memorable as dizzy Tiffany dodging bullets with 007 in Hamilton's *Diamonds Are Forever* (1971), has looked sensational in movies for 25 years, has had two millionaire husbands, was on stage at five, is admired by Henry Kissinger, and generally seems to be doing OK. Here with Frank Sinatra in *Tony Rome* (Douglas, 1967).

Suzanne Pleshette (b.1937) was never more marvellous than in Hitchcock's *The Birds* (1963), but got diverted to Disneyland and hasn't had the movies her intelligence deserves. Mostly on television now, she starred in the remake of *Arch of Triumph* (1981) with Maximilian Schell.

Angie Dickinson (b.1931) always gave as good as she got, notably in *Rio Bravo* (Hawks, 1959), *The Killers* (Siegel, 1964), and *Point Blank* (Boorman, 1967) – pictured here – but is now probably more famous for her dynamic *Police Woman* television series.

Sophia Loren

(b. 1934)

She climbed from nowhere, via beauty contests and modelling, to land bit-parts in Italian movies and careful training from producer Carlo Ponti who, as well as marrying her, got her the starring role alongside Cary Grant and Frank Sinatra in Stanley Kramer's *The Pride and the Passion* (1957). The film was of little account, but Sophia was an instant hit, showing a serene talent for comedy in *The Millionairess* (Asquith, 1960), for medieval fortitude in *El Cid* (Mann, 1961), and for Oscar-winning histrionics in De Sica's *Two Women* (1961). There were some successful comedies with De Sica and occasional ventures abroad (for example, for Chaplin's *Countess from Hong Kong* in 1967), but she then mostly confined her film work to Italy, becoming the taxman's curse and the public's darling.

In her Oscar-winning role in De Sica's *Two Women* (1961).

Accepting a lift in De Sica's *Marriage Italian Style* (1964).

Reporting for duty in De Sica's *Yesterday, Today and Tomorrow* (1964).

In one of the musical sketches from Ettore Giannini's *Neapolitan Fantasy* (1954).

In Arthur Hiller's *Man of La Mancha* (1972).

In Jean Negulesco's *Boy on a Dolphin* (1957).

In Christian-Jaque's *Madame Sans-Gêne* (1962).

Claudia Cardinale

(b. 1939)

She won a beauty competition, appeared at the Venice Film Festival, impressed producer Franco Cristaldi so much that he married her, and had the good sense to choose a hit film for her debut – Mario Monicelli's *Big Deal on Madonna Street* (1958). Since then she's been in much of the best of European cinema. Hollywood productions were safe rather than exciting – *The Pink Panther* (Edwards, 1963), *Circus World* (Hathaway, 1964), *The Professionals* (Brooks, 1966) – but she made three films with Visconti including his masterpiece *The Leopard* (1963), and was the luminous wandering star for Fellini's *Otto e Mezzo* (1963). More recently, as the films continue, she was in Zeffirelli's *Jesus of Nazareth* (1977) and was gracefully maternal in Alan Bridges' *Girl in Blue Velvet* (1978).

In Valerio Zurlini's *Girl with a Suitcase* (1961).

In Pietro Germi's *Un Maledetto Imbroglio* (1959).

In Mikhail Kalatozov's *The Red Tent* (1970).

With Alain Delon in Luchino Visconti's *The Leopard* (1963).

With George Chakiris in Luigi Commencini's *Bebo's Girl* (1963).

As the director's fantasy in Fellini's *Otto e Mezzo* (1963).

Jeanne Moreau

(b. 1928)

There were times when her face would sag into pouches of dejection, others when those same features could glow with a blithe radiance. Her films were frequently concerned with the two extremes and their effect on her admirers; in Demy's *Baie des Anges* (1963), for example, in which she was a compulsive Riviera gambler, the roulette wheel itself determined whether she sulked or shone. A stage actress, her first film was at 30; linked almost by accident with the New Wave in Malle's first films *L'Ascenseur pour l'Echafaud* (1958) and *Les Amants* (1958), she became a central figure in European cinema with Truffaut's *Jules et Jim* (1962), her carefree self-destructiveness being explored by Antonioni, Brook, and Losey (*Eva*, 1962). In De Broca's *Chère Louise* (1972) and in Fassbinder's final film *Querelle* (1982), the same hypnotic contrasts endure.

With Marcello Mastroianni in Antonioni's *La Notte* (1961).

The perfect crime goes wrong in Malle's *L'Ascenseur pour l'Echafaud* (1958).

With Jean-Paul Belmondo in
Peter Brook's *Moderato
Cantabile* (1960).

With Jean-Marc Bory in Louis
Malle's *Les Amants* (1958).

As the elusive heroine of
François Truffaut's *Jules et Jim*
(1962).

With Nino Castelnuovo in Jacques Demy's *Les Parapluies de Cherbourg* (1963).

Catherine Deneuve

(b. 1943)

As the unguarded heroine of Demy's musical romance *Les Parapluies de Cherbourg* (1963) she will always be associated with Michel Legrand's cascading score. In those days, another Vadim discovery in Bardot's wake, she had an inadvertent sensuality masked by an inscrutable calm. She was quickly transformed into a paranoid victim for Polanski's *Repulsion* (1965), and Buñuel found the implications of inferno beneath her icy exterior ideal for *Belle de Jour* (1967) and *Tristana* (1970). Although Demy could still identify the former innocence in his enchanting fairy-tale *Peau d'Ane* (1970), she's now much-travelled and, as can be seen from *Le Dernier Metro* and Tony Scott's *The Hunger* (1982), very much in control.

With Jean Sorel in Luis Buñuel's *Belle de Jour* (1967).

With Mastroianni in Nadine Trintignant's *Ça N'Arrive qu'aux Autres* (1971).

With her sister Françoise Dorléac (*left*) in Demy's *Les Demoiselles de Rochefort* (1967).

In François Truffaut's *Le Dernier Metro* (1980).

195

Melina Mercouri

(b.1923)

As much a part of Greece as the Elgin Marbles, she too has travelled widely, but spends more time in her homeland now the politics are congenial. Her first film was *Stella* (Cacoyannis, 1955), in which her outbursts as a wronged café singer caught the eye of Jules Dassin, in exile from the Hollywood blacklist. He cast her in his allegorical *Celui qui Doit Mourir*, then in his adaptation of Vailland's *La Loi* (1960), and as the effervescent rabble-rouser of *Never on Sunday* (1960), which won her an Oscar nomination. Filming internationally in the 1960s, her greatest role from 1977 became that of Greece's Minister for Culture and Sciences.

With Pierre Vaneck in Dassin's *Celui qui Doit Mourir* (1957).

With Anthony Perkins in Dassin's *Phaedra* (1962).

With Jules Dassin in *Never on Sunday* (1960).

With Peter Finch, Romy Schneider in Dassin's *10.30 p.m. Summer* (1966).

Anna Karina

(b.1940)

Another of the essential faces of the New Wave, her story was told by Godard in the course of his desperate and lyrical movies of the 1960s, beginning with the sequence in *Le Petit Soldat* (filmed in 1960, released in 1963) when everything stops so that she and her flowing hair can be lovingly photographed. Her hairstyles themselves an evocation of Hollywood history (the Louise Brooks style, for example, in *Vivre sa Vie*), she was rescued from 'dehumanization' in *Alphaville* (in 1965, when Godard was trying to win her back) only to be set free in *Pierrot le Fou*, one of the cinema's great love stories, later that same year. She also worked for Vadim, Rivette, Richardson, Cukor. But while she was always welcome, she was no longer spellbound.

With Eddie Constantine in the city of *Alphaville* (Godard, 1965).

As the prostitute Nana in *Vivre sa Vie* (Godard, 1962).

With Jean-Paul Belmondo in *Pierrot le Fou* (Godard, 1965).

Julie Christie

(b. 1941)

A tranquil and amply-proportioned blonde, she seemed in the 1960s to be the answer to the chauvinist's dream, fresh from another planet in television's *A for Andromeda* (1962), the fantasy creation for *Billy Liar* (Schlesinger, 1963), and the vision of perfection for *Doctor Zhivago*. She won the Oscar for *Darling* (Schlesinger, 1965), written specially for her, and could have stayed the uncomplaining goddess for years if common sense hadn't intervened, brought her back to earth, and rendered her activist and innovative, working in low-budget films like Gladwell's *Memoirs of a Survivor* (1981) and Sally Potter's *The Gold Diggers* (1983). Fortunately she sometimes still ventures into more traditional territory like Ivory's *Heat and Dust* (1982).

With Rod Steiger in David Lean's *Doctor Zhivago* (1965).

As the anxious Lara, confronting Alec Guinness in *Doctor Zhivago*.

Vanessa Redgrave

(b.1937)

The famous name and the family skills are teamed in her with an urgent, nervous presence, as if she were prepared to sacrifice her integrity but never her beliefs in order to win the next round of the campaign. The political causes have paralleled the cinematic sacrifices throughout her career, and hers is an uncomfortable kind of stardom, captivating in *Camelot* (Logan, 1967), daft in *The Devils* (Russell, 1971), agonising in *Agatha* (Apted, 1979), and fully justified in *Julia*, which won her an Oscar (there had also been Oscar nominations for her films with Karel Reisz: *Morgan: A Suitable Case for Treatment* in 1966, and *Isadora* in 1968). When the message and the medium are right, as for her prizewinning role in Arthur Miller's *Playing for Time* (Mann, 1981), she's formidable.

In Fred Zinnemann's *Julia* (1977).

With Jane Fonda in the Oscar-winning *Julia*.

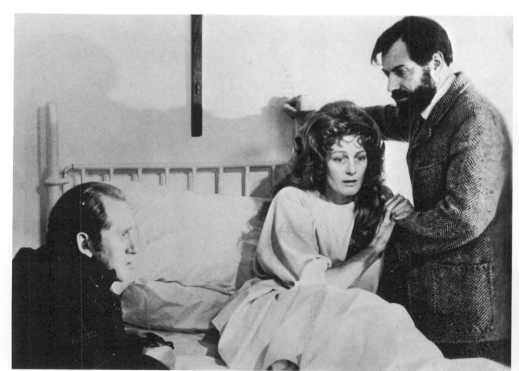

With Nicol Williamson and Alan Arkin in *The Seven-Percent Solution* (Herbert Ross, 1976).

With Sean Connery in Lumet's *Murder on the Orient Express* (1974).

As Isadora Duncan in Karel Reisz's *Isadora* (1968).

Romy Schneider *(1938-1982)* was in nearly 60 films in an international career that began in Austria in 1953; she worked with Welles (*The Trial*, 1962), Preminger (*The Cardinal*, 1963), Visconti (*Ludwig*, 1973), Losey, Chabrol, and was probably at her finest in five films by Claude Sautet. Here with Jean-Louis Trintignant in *L'Important C'Est d'Aimer* (Granier-Deferre, 1974).

Elke Sommer *(b.1940)*, multilingual sex-kitten, was very much the saucy Continental star in Hollywood dramas of the 1960s, with Paul Newman (*above*) in Mark Robson's *The Prize* (1963), and with Peter Sellers in *A Shot in the Dark* (Edwards, 1964).

Irene Papas *(b.1926)*; built for the classic tragedies, she has been Electra (1962), Helen (1971) and Iphigenia (1977) for Cacoyannis, but was also memorable in *The Guns of Navarone* (Thompson, 1961) and *Zorba the Greek* (Cacoyannis, 1964).

Catherine Spaak (b.1945), daughter of scenarist Charles Spaak, sister to the Belgian premier and to actress Agnès, she was in films at 15 with Lattuada's *I Dolci Inganni* (1960) and was a trouble to the censors from then on. Here with Maurice Ronet in Vadim's *La Ronde* (1960).

Stéphane Audran (b.1932), marvellously poised and subtle star of husband Claude Chabrol's many films; first noticed as one of the shop-girls in *Les Bonnes Femmes* (1960), she has occasionally worked for other directors like Buñuel and Sam Fuller. Here as the deceiving bourgeois wife in Chabrol's *La Femme Infidèle* (1968).

Elsa Martinelli (b.1935); picked by Kirk Douglas from an impoverished background to her first film in 1955, she regularly enhanced the European cinema of the 1960s but was at her best in Howard Hawks' *Hatari!* (1962), coping with John Wayne and the other wildlife.

Monica Vitti (b.1931), became Antonioni's infinitely forgiving heroine in *L'Avventura* (1960), impersonates the exotic special agent *Modesty Blaise* for Losey in 1966, and was soon Italy's favourite comedienne; her own film, *Flirt*, won Best Actress Award at Berlin in 1984.

Hayley Mills *(b.1946)*, seen here with Maureen O'Hara in her Disney hit *The Parent Trap* (Swift, 1961), was a revelation at 12 in *Tiger Bay* (Thompson, 1959), but had problems with an older image and settled for television.

Rachel Roberts *(1927-1980)* became the grand lady of kitchen-sink drama with Reisz's *Saturday Night and Sunday Morning* (1960) and Anderson's *This Sporting Life* (1963), which won her an Oscar nomination.

Delphine Seyrig *(b.1932)* was languid and forgetful in *L'Année Dernière à Marienbad* (Resnais, 1961), but changed the style delightfully for Truffaut, Buñuel, Losey, Demy and many others.

Marie Laforêt *(b.1941)*; spellbinding singer and wistfully meditative actress, she was Albicocco's *Girl with the Golden Eyes* (1960). Here with Alain Delon in René Clément's thriller *Plein Soleil* (1960).

Mireille Darc (b.1938), perhaps best known outside France for Godard's *Weekend* (1967) and Deray's *Blood on the Streets* (1974), she has been both prolific and unlucky in her career. Here with Delon in *Madly*, which she wrote (Kahane, 1970).

Nathalie Delon (b.1941), once termed 'the most talked-about woman in Europe', looked stunning with husband Alain in Melville's *Le Samourai* (1967), made her own film *Ils Appellent Ça un Accident* (1982), and lives in the Caribbean.

Susannah York (b.1941); one of RADA's finest, she's been just about everywhere, in films by Aldrich, Huston, Skolimowski, and with an Oscar nomination for *They Shoot Horses Don't They?* (Pollack, 1969). Here in J. Lee Thompson's *Country Dance* (1969).

Lila Kedrova (b.1918), Russian-born piano-playing prodigy on stage at 15, in films early 1950s, worked for Hitchcock, Polanski, Huston; won her Oscar supporting Anthony Quinn in *Zorba the Greek* (Cacoyannis, 1964).

203

Tatiana Samoilova (b.1934), seen here in her world-wide hit *The Cranes are Flying* (Kalatozov, 1957), was never able to find anything to match its impact, but was an appealing *Anna Karenina* (Sarchi, 1968).

Luciana Paluzzi (b.1937), after *Three Coins in the Fountain* (Negulesco, 1954), made a lovely adversary to 007 in *Thunderball* (Young, 1965) and was also found in tatty Italian co-productions.

Mai Zetterling (b.1925) came to attention in *Frenzy* (Sjöberg, 1944), was in British films like *Seven Waves Away* (Sale, 1957) and *Only Two Can Play* (Gilliat, 1961), and graduated to quirky film-making with *Loving Couples* (1964) and *Scrubbers* (1982).

Annie Girardot (b.1931), has been a mainstay of European cinema since her anguished role in *Rocco and his Brothers* (Visconti, 1960), notably with Ferreri's *The Ape Woman* (1964), and Lelouch's *Vivre pour Vivre* (1967).

THE 1970s

In the 1970s, as if to punish its fickle audience, the cinema abandoned restraint. In the wake of *Bonnie and Clyde*, deaths on screen were ever more intricate and repellent. The aspiring actress might find herself on a meat-hook or under a chainsaw at any moment. Either way, she was likely to be mere raw material, soon lost and forgotten among the credits. Disaster was in the air and under the feet. If the earthquakes and the towering infernos didn't get you, the jaws were waiting. In reminder of what was lost, nostalgia arrived at all levels. For younger audiences, *American Graffiti* recaptured the golden days of rock'n'pop; for the older generation, *That's Entertainment* illustrated how blessedly simple the classic musicals had been. If you were an established name in this decade, guest appearances were remunerative. If you were just starting, it was the very devil to get noticed. But as the following pages amply demonstrate, there was still plenty of talent around.

Jane Fonda

(b.1937)

It was a slow beginning in Logan's *Tall Story* (1960), followed by tepid shockers like Cukor's *The Chapman Report* (1962), but Vadim gave her image a sense of fun in *Barbarella* (1968), France gave her a sense of politics, and she veered between anti-Vietnam protest in *F.T.A.* (Parker, 1972) and the Oscar-winning *Klute*. Now, thanks to *Julia*, Pakula's *Comes a Horseman* (1978), Bridges' *China Syndrome* (1979), *9 to 5*, and the elegiac *On Golden Pond* (Rydell, 1981), 'Hanoi Jane' has become the epitome of healthy U.S. womanhood.

With Alain Delon in René Clément's *The Love Cage* (1964).

With Michael Sarrazin in *They Shoot Horses, Don't They?* (Pollack, 1969).

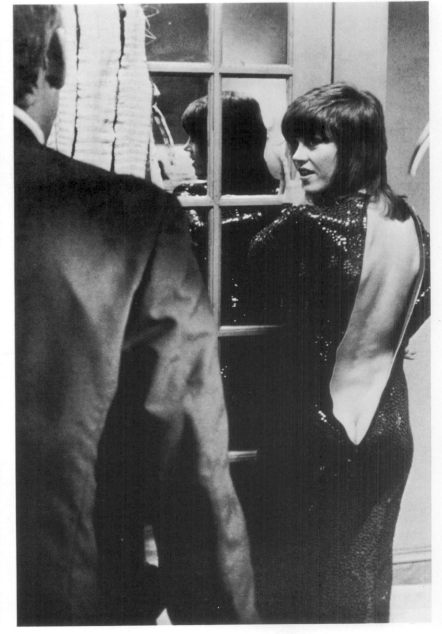

With Donald Sutherland in Alan Pakula's *Klute* (1971).

In Joseph Losey's film of Ibsen's *A Doll's House* (1973), in the role of Nora.

In Fred Zinnemann's *Julia* (1977).

As the nervously rebellious secretary in Colin Higgins' *9 to 5* (1980).

Faye Dunaway

(b. 1941)

Not long to live in Vittorio De Sica's *A Place for Lovers* (1968).

Her image is of the go-getting kind, making her a not inappropriate reincarnation of Joan Crawford for Frank Perry's loudly biographical *Mommie Dearest* (1981). A hustling, awesome businesswoman in *The Eyes of Laura Mars* (Kershner, 1978) and *Network*, she has acquired a ruthless glitter that makes one fear the worst. It seems a far cry already from the small-town irresponsibilities of *Bonnie and Clyde*, as though that paradise-lost account of a girl betrayed had left its brightly blood-soaked star with some grim scores to settle. But the slightly hooded eyes and the despairing gasp of the mouth in the pale and luminous face also maintain an aura of imminent deprivation so that, as for Bonnie, a tragic end seems bound to loom over every Dunaway story. Small wonder that despite the surefire comic timing of her contributions to *Little Big Man* (Penn, 1970) and Lester's films of the Musketeers (1973 and 1975), audiences for Zeffirelli's *The Champ* (1979) came prepared to swim for their lives through a vale of tears.

With Kirk Douglas in Elia Kazan's *The Arrangement* (1969).

Neurosis, incest and gunplay in Polanski's *Chinatown* (1974).

With Warren Beatty in Arthur Penn's *Bonnie and Clyde* (1967).

As television producer in Sidney Lumet's *Network* (1976).

With Ricky Schroder in Franco Zeffirelli's remake of *The Champ* (1979).

Barbra Streisand

(b.1942)

Former switchboard operator, nightclub singer, and Broadway star, she claimed an Oscar with her first film, Wyler's *Funny Girl* (1968), sharing the award – symbolically enough – with Katharine Hepburn. So much praise has followed, including a 1970 Tony for being considered the best actress of the decade, and so many show-stopping blockbusters like *Hello, Dolly!*, *Funny Lady* (Ross, 1975), and *A Star is Born* (Pierson, 1976), that her very own *Yentl* (1983), although constructed with care and originality, seemed almost an anticlimax.

With Omar Sharif in William Wyler's *Funny Girl* (1968).

With Walter Matthau in Gene Kelly's *Hello, Dolly!* (1969).

With Robert Redford in Sydney Pollack's *The Way We Were* (1973).

In her Oscar-winning role – Sally Bowles
as nightclub entertainer in *Cabaret*.

Liza Minnelli

(b. 1946)

Given her parents, nothing could
keep her out of showbusiness.
And nothing was likely to make it
an easy path to take. Her early
elfin charm first seen at the age of
three in Leonard's *In the Good Old
Summertime* (1949), she was a
pleasure in Albert Finney's
Charlie Bubbles (1967) but rather
mannered by the time of *New
York, New York* (1977). The high-
spot has of course been *Cabaret*,
which caught her nightclub skills at
just the right moment – larger
than life, nowhere near as natural,
and resplendently decadent.

As Sally Bowles in Christopher Isherwood's story for Bob Fosse's *Cabaret* (1972); *(right)* with Robert De Niro in Scorsese's *New York, New York* (1977).

Karen Black

(b.1943)

In John Flynn's *The Outfit* (1973).

After a Best Actress Award on Broadway, she made it into movies with Coppola's *You're a Big Boy Now* (1966) and became associated with hungry, intense, and unorthodox roles in off-beat subjects like *Easy Rider* (Hopper, 1969), *Drive, He Said* (Nicholson, 1971) and *Portnoy's Complaint* (Lehman, 1972). Her prize for *Five Easy Pieces* led to more mainstream work but didn't deflect her from taking risks with films like Altman's *Nashville* (1975) and *Come Back to the 5 and Dime, Jimmy Dean, Jimmy Dean* (1982), in which she had a richly ambiguous part and rivetingly made the most of it.

With Charlton Heston in Jack Smight's *Airport '75* (1974).

In Bob Rafelson's *Five Easy Pieces* (1970).

With William Devane in Hitchcock's *Family Plot* (1976).

Diane Keaton

(b.1946)

As Al Pacino's wife in *The Godfather* (Coppola, 1972-4) watching her U.S. serviceman husband turn into a Mafia boss, she had an air of incredulity that the well-ordered world could contain such chaos. The sense of disbelief stayed with her in the Woody Allen era, her expressions of mingled scorn and curiosity winning her an Oscar for *Annie Hall* in 1977. After the nightmarish *Looking for Mr Goodbar* (Brooks, 1977), she acquired a sadder and wiser presence, effortlessly dominating *Shoot the Moon*, and earning an Oscar nomination for *Reds*.

As Louise Bryant, reporting the Bolshevik Revolution in Warren Beatty's *Reds* (1981).

With Woody Allen, her director for six films; (*right*) with Alan Parker during the filming of *Shoot the Moon* (1982).

Candice Bergen (b. 1946), former model and photojournalist, overcame the general consensus (with which she amiably agreed for a while) that she couldn't act by turning in high-gloss performances in Pakula's *Starting Over* (1979) and Cukor's *Rich and Famous* (1981).

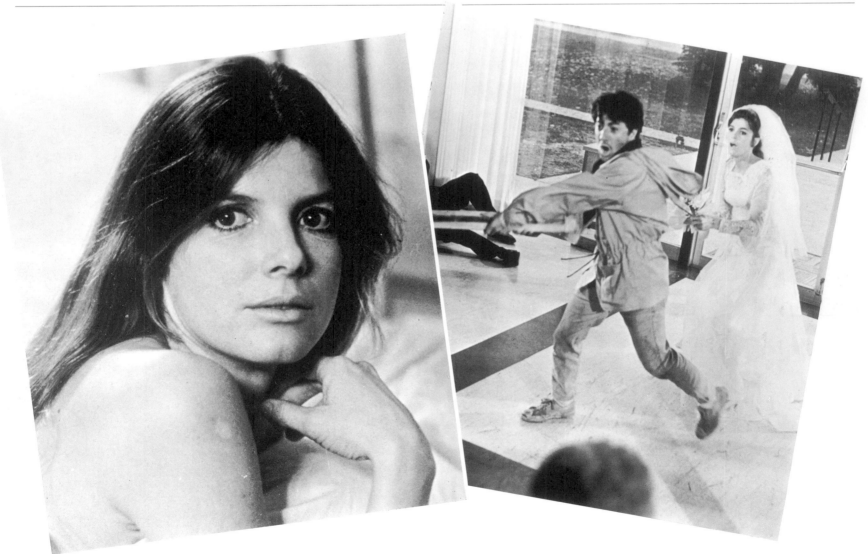

Katharine Ross (b. 1943), admirably suited to be the outrageously perfect woman of Bryan Forbes' *The Stepford Wives* (1975), seems to have become typecast in mechanical roles following her resounding debut as a bride worth stealing from any altar in Mike Nichols' *The Graduate* (1967) – pictured here with Dustin Hoffman, winning herself an Oscar nomination.

Ali McGraw (b.1938), ex-cover-girl who found herself widely disliked for doing a good job in an unlikeable part in the monumental *Winds of War* series (1983), looked aggressively healthy in Arthur Hiller's *Love Story* (1970) – pictured here with Ray Milland – and aggressively desirable in Peckinpah's *The Getaway* (1972) alongside Steve McQueen, and *Convoy* (1978) in convoy with Kris Kristofferson.

Jennifer O'Neill (b.1948), ex-*Vogue* model who had a hit with Robert Mulligan's *Summer of '42* (1971), always gives reliable performances in surprising contexts, like Visconti's *L'Innocente* (1976) and Cronenberg's *Scanners* (1981).

Sally Kellerman (b.1938), nominated for an Oscar for being 'Hot Lips' Houlihan in Altman's *M.A.S.H.* (1970), retired from films for nightclub work, but returned for Hill's *A Little Romance* (1979) and Smight's *Loving Couples* (1980).

Tatum O'Neal (*b.1963*) won her Oscar at ten for appearing with father Ryan O'Neal in Peter Bogdanovich's *Paper Moon* (1973) as an orphan teamed with a Bible-selling con-man. Paid a record fee in 1976 for Michael Ritchie's *The Bad News Bears* (*above left*, with Walter Matthau), she grew up respectably for *International Velvet* (Forbes, 1978) and disreputably for *Little Darlings* (Maxwell, 1980), in which she strove to seduce Armand Assante (*left*).

Kristy McNichol (*b.1962*) was in television series and commercials as a child, had hit records with brother Jimmy, and made movies from 1977, notably with Tatum O'Neal in *Little Darlings* and as the owner of the racist Alsatian in Sam Fuller's *White Dog* (1981).

Linda Blair (*b.1959*), former child model, lost out to Tatum O'Neal for an Oscar for *The Exorcist* (Friedkin, 1973), was even better in Boorman's under-rated *Exorcist II: The Heretic* (1977), had a fiendish private life, and not surprisingly finds the image hard to change.

Marsha Mason *(b.1942)*; stage actress nominated for Oscar for *Cinderella Liberty* (Rydell, 1973), she married Neil Simon and personified his quickfire comedy style in Herbert Ross's *The Goodbye Girl* (1977) *left*, with Richard Dreyfuss, *The Cheap Detective* (Moore, 1978), and *Chapter Two* (Moore, 1979).

Susan Clark *(b.1940)*; now widely appreciated as Cherry Forever in *Porky's* (Clark, 1981), she has been an attractive feature of a broad range of movies since teaming with Siegel and Eastwood in 1968 for *Madigan* and *Coogan's Bluff*, as well as for Joseph Sargent's superb *The Forbin Project* (1969). Shown here in Edwin Sherin's *Valdez is Coming* (1971).

Mary Steenburgen *(b.1954)*; whether coping with Dudley Moore in *Romantic Comedy* (Hiller, 1983) or Rip Torn in the swamps of *Cross Creek* (Ritt, 1982), she shows the same slightly distracted determination as when Jack Nicholson discovered her for *Goin' South* (1978).

Shelley Duvall *(b.1949)*; a regular in Altman movies, such as *Thieves Like Us* (1974) and *Nashville* (1975), she won a Best Actress prize at Cannes for *Three Women* (1977). Her gawky air of apprehension was ideal for Kubrick's *The Shining* (1980).

Gena Rowlands *(b. 1936)*, wife of actor-director John Cassavetes, wins prizes in his movies, including *A Woman Under the Influence* (1974), *Gloria* (*above*) in 1980, and *Love Streams* (1984).

Ellen Burstyn *(b. 1932)*, good in anything, gets Tony awards on stage, Oscar nominations on screen, winning with Scorsese's *Alice Doesn't Live Here Anymore* (1974).

Jodie Foster *(b. 1963)*, inadvertently a part of U.S. history, started in commercials at three, appeared in *Gunsmoke*, was a knockout in *Taxi Driver* (Scorsese, 1976) and *Bugsy Malone* (Parker, 1976), and is still growing. Seen here with Kandice Stroh, Marilyn Kagan and (on right) Cherie Currie in *Foxes* (Lyne, 1980).

Barbara Harris *(b.1937)*, Broadway director and actress, has a nice line in comedy whether Disney (Nelson's *Freaky Friday*, 1976) or off-beat (Brooks' *Movie Movie*, 1978); here with Bruce Dern in Hitchcock's last film *Family Plot* (1976).

Marthe Keller *(b.1945)*; beguiling and mysterious Swiss actress who, via *Funeral in Berlin* (Hamilton, 1966), reached Hollywood and pivotal roles in *Marathon Man* (Schlesinger, 1976), *Black Sunday* (Frankenheimer, 1977), and Pollack's *Bobby Deerfield* (1977), here with Al Pacino.

Brooke Shields *(b.1965)*; with soap commercials and parental guidance one of the top U.S. infant models, she was in films at 12 being murdered in *Alice, Sweet Alice* (Sole, 1976), and distressed everybody as a child prostitute *(above)* in Malle's *Pretty Baby* (1978). Destined for the sultry stuff, she looks fresh out of school in *Endless Love* (Zeffirelli, 1981) and *Sahara* (McLaglen, 1983), but still has much to learn.

Meryl Streep (b.1950), with an impeccable pedigree as a Shakespearian actress, made her first screen appearance in *Julia* (Zinnemann, 1977). Demonstrably able to play anything from Victorian heroine (*above*, with Jeremy Irons, in Reisz's *French Lieutenant's Woman* in 1981) to anti-nuclear activist, and with two Oscars already (for Benton's *Kramer vs Kramer* in 1979, and (*right*) Pakula's *Sophie's Choice* in 1982), she's at the top of her profession.

Jill Clayburgh (b.1944), with her air of anxious honesty, made a delightful divorcee in Mazursky's *An Unmarried Woman* (1978), which gained an Oscar nomination, and in Pakula's *Starting Over* (1979).

Farrah Fawcett (b.1947) was the best-selling Charlie's Angel of 1976, set a new trend in hairstyles, but was undistinguished in *Sunburn* (Sarafian, 1979) and *Saturn 3* (Donen, 1980).

Jessica Lange (b.1950), seen here with Jack Nicholson in *The Postman Always Rings Twice* (Rafelson, 1981), only just survived the second *King Kong* (Guillermin, 1976) but was Oscar-winning in *Tootsie* (Pollack, 1983).

Goldie Hawn (b.1945), once a dancing teacher, was the best part of the *Laugh-in* television series in the 1960s as a cheeky feather-brain; but once she got into movies she proved she could act too, notably in her Oscar-winning *Cactus Flower* (Saks, 1969) and in Spielberg's *Sugarland Express* (1974).

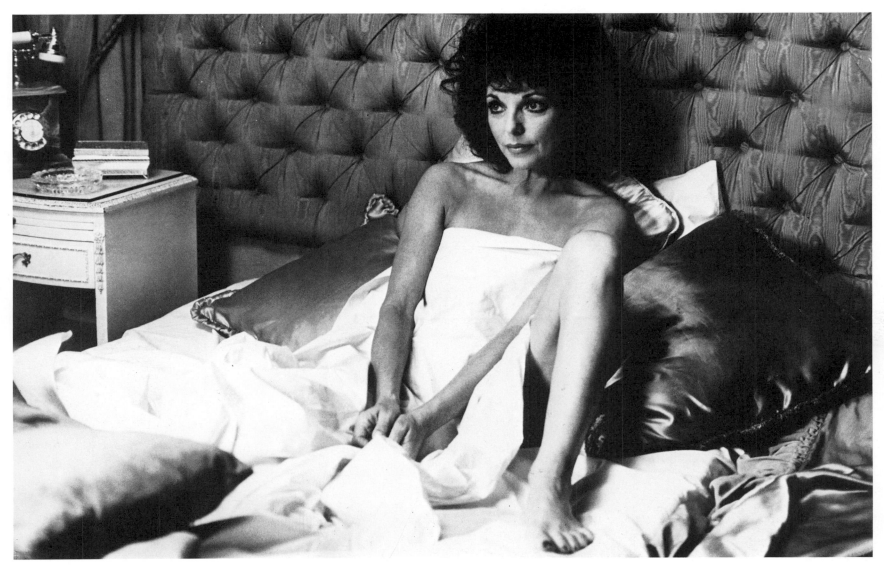

Joan Collins (b.1933) always raised the temperature in British crime thrillers of the 1950s, usually as a prominent delinquent and then went to Hollywood to pose decoratively in epics like *Land of the Pharaohs* (Hawks, 1955). Unaffected by the passing years, she now blisters the paintwork in films like *The Stud* (Masters, 1978) and *Nutcracker* (Kawadri, 1982), and as superbitch Alexis in the television series *Dynasty*.

Brigitte Fossey *(b.1947)* was the little girl in René Clément's *Les Jeux Interdits* (1952) when she was only five (*above left*, with George Poujouly), specialized in languages and philosophy, and returned to the screen in another classic, Albicocco's *Le Grand Meaulnes* (1967); now established on French stage and television, she was also in Altman's *Quintet* (1979).

Glenda Jackson *(b.1936)*, matter-of-fact and firmly non-glamorous on stage or screen, is usually the modern woman who, while conscious of her imperfections, strives to be true to her own identity. Oscars for *Women in Love* (Russell, 1969) and *A Touch of Class* (Frank, 1973), and classic roles in Schlesinger's *Sunday, Bloody, Sunday* (1971), and Losey's *The Romantic Englishwoman* (1975).

Sarah Miles *(b.1932)*, always seemingly on the brink of tears, has had an erratic and troubled career but was at her best for Losey in *The Servant* (1963) and Lean in *Ryan's Daughter* (1970) *above*, with Christopher Jones. For her then husband, Robert Bolt, she played *Lady Caroline Lamb* (1972).

Charlotte Rampling *(b.1946)* has a lean and hungry look, and eyelids as heavy as Mitchum's with whom she starred in Dick Richards' admirable remake of *Farewell, My Lovely* (1975). She was also dramatic in *Zardoz* (Boorman, 1974) and *The Verdict* (Lumet, 1982).

Françoise Fabian *(b.1934)* was the glossy, imperturbable star of Eric Rohmer's *Ma Nuit Chez Maud* (1969) and specializes in sophisticated dramas like Lelouch's *La Bonne Année* (1973) which won her a Best Actress award at San Sebastian.

Liv Ullmann *(b.1939)* was the star of Bergman's *Persona* (1966) and despite visits to Hollywood for oddities like *Pope Joan* (Anderson, 1972) and *Lost Horizon* (Jarrott, 1973) continued to look best in Bergman works like *Cries and Whispers* (1972), pictured here with frequent co-star Erland Josephson.

Sydne Rome *(b.1946)* began her film career in 1968 with Ralph Thomas' *Some Girls Do*, and was then in 22 films in eight years, notably Polanski's *What?* (1972) and for a celebrated nude scene in *Just a Gigolo* (Hemmings, 1978).

Jacqueline Bisset (b.1944) went from private school to London Lycée to photographic model, and was one of Ray Brooks' many fans in Dick Lester's *The Knack* (1965). Roles in *Cul-de-Sac* (Polanski, 1966) and *Two for the Road* (Donen, 1966) then led to a Fox contract and a good quantity of self-possessed showings, including (*left*) *Secret World* (Freeman, 1969) and (*right*) Truffaut's *Day for Night* (1973) with Jean-Pierre Léaud.

Geraldine Chaplin (b.1944) was set for the Royal Ballet until her performance in *Doctor Zhivago* (1965) showed she was too good an actress not to escape her father's shadow. Equally at home in films by Altman or by Carlos Saura, she's seen here in (*left*) Nelo Risi's *Andremo in Città* (1965) and (*right*) Claude Lelouch's *Les Uns et les Autres* (1981).

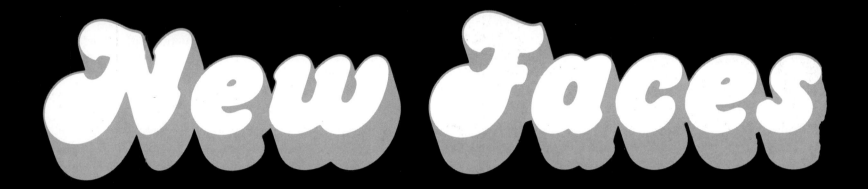

New Faces

The *Star Wars* generation is long on hardware, short on the humanities, but with aerobic-supple militancy the better half is fighting back. And these are, or could be, or should be, the stars who will have helped to enrich the final dozen of the cinema's first 100 years. Between them, they have already created some remarkable movies. And they are the most vital signs and meanings the cinema has ever offered – not because (as it was with Garbo) they must represent a million impossible dreams, but because they are demonstrably participants, equal shareholders. Emerging from the everyday, they show that movies are like any other kind of work. Anybody can do it, and stardom no longer needs the camera for confirmation. Some of these faces, as has so often happened before, may never be seen again, although they all deserve some lasting recognition. But whether on film or tape or disc, movies couldn't exist without the spirit and the courage they represent.

Nastassia Kinski *(b.1961)*

Fortunately the resemblance to her father, the cadaverous, tortured Herzog hero, is only fleeting. Doubtless the Kinski heritage can be glimpsed from time to time in her restless manner and the contemplative melancholy of her gaze; through the eyes, the past seems fraught with disquieting truths, the future a promise of persistent disillusion. Her face is a perfect mirror for the malaise of the 1980s, and she's one of the hottest properties in the world's movie business; according to Polanski, who encountered her at 15, she also has a will of steel.

After an education in Rome, Munich and Caracas, she took drama courses with Lee Strasberg in her early teens, and made her first screen appearance in 1975 in Wim Wenders' *Wrong Movement*, followed by a horror film, an Italo-Spanish co-production, and weeks of training in Dorset accents for *Tess*. Once considered for Jennifer Jones, then for Sharon Tate, the role was fully to her liking; in interviews, she identified with Hardy's heroine completely, often casting Polanski as D'Urberville, a latter-day Svengali.

Tess's guilty sensuality was easily transferred to the role of Irena in *Cat People* (1982), although the special effects inevitably stole the best of her performance. As the fashion

As Irena in Paul Schrader's remake of the Tourneur classic *Cat People* (1982).

226

model in Toback's *Exposed* (1982), as much a celebration of Jean-Pierre Melville's Paris as of Nastassia herself, she was played by Nureyev like an instrument and looked suitably vibrant. And she was exploited superbly by the floating camera of Beineix in *The Moon in the Gutter* (1983), a far finer film than generally credited, which turned the elusive David Goodis rich-girl tease into an authentic princess of the night, all mystery and provocation. Never staying put, with films for Richardson, Schamoni, Zieff and others already adding to her output, Nastassia claims to be fatalistic but is clearly giving fate a run for its money.

As Thomas Hardy's tragic heroine in Roman Polanski's *Tess* (1979).

As the mysterious Loretta Channing in Jean-Jacques Beineix's *The Moon in the Gutter* (1983).

Sigourney Weaver (b. 1949) as Ripley, warrant officer of the spacecraft Nostromo in Ridley Scott's *Alien* (1979).

Director Ridley Scott's habit of encouraging his cast to fill in the details of their characterisations worked out fine for at least two of his actresses with plenty of detail to provide. **Sigourney Weaver** was in off-Broadway plays when invited to audition for *Alien*; she contributed so much power and authority to being the one human survivor of the besieged spacecraft that it was a short step to similarly resourceful roles in *Eyewitness* (Yates, 1981) and *The Year of Living Dangerously* (Weir, 1982).

For **Joanna Cassidy**, the role in *Blade Runner* which enabled her to reveal an impressive physique (during filming she's up at 4.30 a.m. for weight-training) was another rung on a career ladder that began with modelling and commercials and bit-parts in *Starsky & Hutch* and *Dallas*. She was in movies like Benton's *The Late Show* (1977); and now her subtle and energetic performance in *Under Fire* (Spottiswoode, 1983) promises even better moves ahead.

Joanna Cassidy *(b.1946)* as Zhora, replicant nightclub entertainer, in Ridley Scott's *Blade Runner* (1982).

Mariel Hemingway (b.1962) as *Playboy* Playmate Dorothy Stratten in Bob Fosse's *Star 80* (1983).

Bulle Ogier (b.1939) as Viviane in
Barbet Schroeder's *La Vallée*
(1972).

Kim Basinger (b.1954) as Domino in Irvin Kershner's *Never Say Never Again* (1983).

Youngest granddaughter of the novelist, **Mariel Hemingway** was more interested in skiing than movies when at 13 she helped elder sister Margaux in *Lipstick* (Johnson, 1976). Woody Allen then picked her for *Manhattan* (1979), and despite her shyness and inexperience she was such a hit that she began to take acting seriously. She fought to prove herself suitable for her next two films, training as an athlete for *Personal Best* (Towne, 1982) and giving herself some enhanced dimensions for the contrasting role of *Playboy* pin-up girl in *Star 80*. Both confirmed her very exciting potential as an actress.

From fringe theatre, **Bulle Ogier** first worked in the cinema for Jacques Rivette, one of the finest New Wave directors, who cast her in *L'Amour Fou* (1968) and four later films. Cool and level-headed but with a touch of dreaminess, she has conveyed the extremes of sensuality for Barbet Schroeder's *La Vallée* and *Maîtresse* (1976) and of naivety for Tanner's *La Salamandre* (1971) and De Gregorio's *Les Papiers d'Aspern* (1982). Seemingly happiest working round the edges of society – a bank robber in Molinaro's *Hostages* (1973), a near-hippie in Buñuel's *Discreet Charm of the Bourgeoisie* (1973) – she has been in three films by the experimentalist Marguerite Duras.

Arriving from nowhere to be 007's richly decorative partner in *Never Say Never Again*, **Kim Basinger** has in fact been working her way steadily to stardom. Top New York model in the 1970s, she packed up and went to Hollywood, appeared in *Six Million Dollar Man* and *Charlie's Angels* and as *Katie: Portrait of a Centrefold* (1978) – a television role she turned to reality by baring all in *Playboy* in 1982 – and captured national interest in the television mini-series *From Here to Eternity* (1980). Her movie debut was David Greene's *Hard Country* (1980); then came Charlton Heston's *Mother Lode* (1982), the Bond film, Blake Edwards' *The Man Who Loved Women* (1984), and Robert Redford's *The Natural* (1984). On her records, she's known as Chelsa.

At the centre of *Camelot*, **Cherie Lunghi** brought an ethereal and crystalline beauty to Boorman's *Excalibur* (1981). A Pre-Raphaelite fantasy come true, she's tougher than you'd suppose, with stage roles from Chekhov to Shakespeare, and on television in everything from Molière to Agatha Christie. Once in shampoo commercials, now she's a brittle wife in C.P. Snow's *Strangers and Brothers* or an incestuous Jacobean in *'Tis Pity She's a Whore*. The big screen, though, is where she belongs.

Dolly Parton has been the Mae West of country music almost since the first radio and television shows at ten, the first Nashville Opry performances at 13. She admits some of the image is fake, although most, like her bubbling personality, is outstandingly genuine. A late but delightful start in movies came with *9 to 5* (Higgins, 1980), and as Sylvester Stallone's counterpart in *Rhinestone Cowboy* (1984) there seems plenty more of her on the way. If that's possible.

Cherie Lunghi (b.1954) as Guinevere in John Boorman's *Excalibur* (1981).

Dolly Parton (b.1946) in *The Best Little Whorehouse in Texas* (Higgins, 1982).

As daughter to Tony Curtis and Janet Leigh, **Jamie Lee Curtis** seemed bound for movies and was under contract to Universal at 19 for a horde of television shows like *Quincy, Columbo,* and *Charlie's Angels*. Savaged by John Carpenter for his smash-hit *Halloween* (1978), she submitted profitably to victimization in such chillers as *The Fog* (1980), *Prom Night* (Lynch, 1980), and *Halloween II* (Rosenthal, 1981) but has emerged safely from the ordeal in the John Landis comedy *Trading Places* (1983) and seems unlikely to have to cringe again.

In films at 14, and on the cover of *Time* magazine in 1977, **Isabelle Adjani** has shown a disconcerting ability to play anything, anywhere. Truffaut made her a star with *L'Histoire d'Adèle H* (1975), Polanski followed up with *The Lodger* (1976), she made an intriguing American debut with Walter Hill's *The Driver* (1978), and won the Best Actress Award at Cannes for Ivory's *Quartet* (1981). Herzog showed her as anaemic, Zulawski as maniacal; she also works at the Comédie Française.

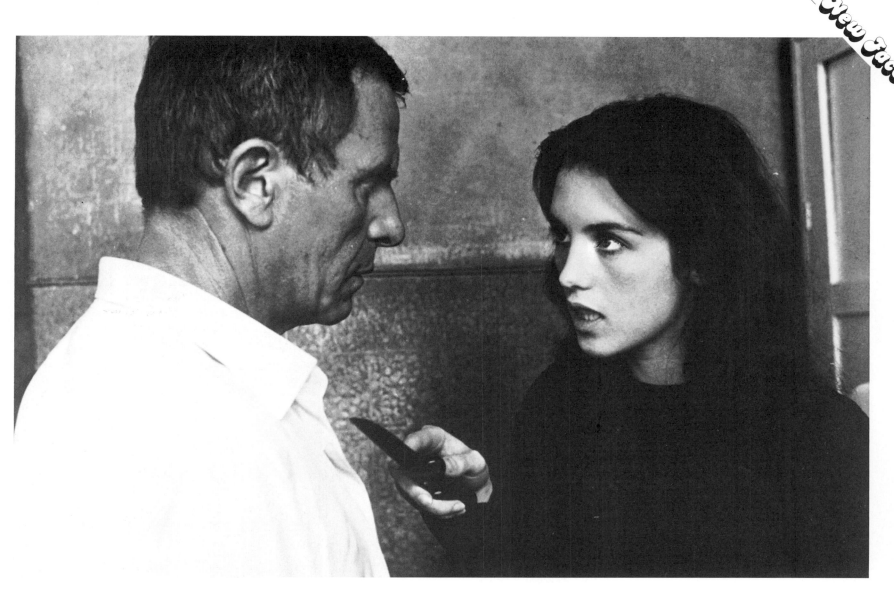

Isabelle Adjani (b.1956) with Heinz Bennent in André Zulawski's *Possession* (1981).

Jamie Lee Curtis (b.1958) with Eddie Murphy (*left*) and Dan Aykroyd in *Trading Places* (Landis, 1983).

Capable of an astonishing range, **Isabelle Huppert** is among the most welcome and frequent faces in the cinema of the 1980s. After drama school in Paris, she was in her first film at 16, *Faustine et le Bel Eté* (Companeez, 1971), and after 14 more films became the tragically docile heroine of *The Lacemaker* (Goretta, 1976). The role of victim who strikes back was developed in Chabrol's *Violette Nozière* (1978), which won her the Best Actress Award at Cannes, but she is more often the uninhibited happy-go-lucky type as in *Loulou* (Pialat, 1979) or Cimino's magnificent *Heaven's Gate* (1979).

After training as a dancer in New York, **Nathalie Baye** took a drama course in Paris and was in bit-parts in movies from 1972, appearing in more than 26 films in the next dozen years. Most notable were Truffaut's *Day for Night* (1973), Ferreri's *The Last Woman* (1976), and Godard's *Sauve qui Peut (La Vie)*, for which she won a César in 1981. Whether as the sixteenth-century wife unsure of her husband's identity in *Le Retour de Martin Guerre* (Vigne, 1981) or as the Paris hooker in Bob Swaim's *La Balance* (1982), she's an authoritative performer.

Clearly born to be a fighter, **Judy Davis** will always be linked with Sybylla, the recalcitrant, unconventional feminist in Gillian Armstrong's *My Brilliant Career* (1979). Courted by Sam Neill, the girl from the Australian outback refuses to take the expected path of marriage, carving out for herself a more hazardous future as a writer. The air of knowing cynicism that Judy brings to the screen has made her an effective champion of any causes going, as when, gun in hand, she battles big business interests in Noyce's *Heatwave* (1981) or, rather more vaguely, the U.S. imperialists in *Who Dares Wins* (Sharp, 1982). A former jazz singer, her brilliant career looks best in costume, as for Lean's *Passage to India* (1984).

Isabelle Huppert (b.1955) as Ella Watson in Michael Cimino's *Heaven's Gate* (1980).

Nathalie Baye *(b.1948)* in Jean-Luc Godard's *Sauve qui Peut (La Vie)* (1981).

Judy Davis *(b.1955)* in Phil Noyce's *Heatwave* (1981).

Hoping for a break into the music industry, she was once a singer-songwriter. Then, guided by cousin Rip Torn and his wife Geraldine Page into the acting profession, **Sissy Spacek** trained with Lee Strasberg and worked in television. Her perpetually teenage features made her a convincing 15-year-old in Michael Ritchie's *Prime Cut* (1972) and Terrence Malick's *Badlands* (1973), she was a frighteningly beleaguered college-girl in De Palma's classic *Carrie* (1976) and Altman's *Three Women* (1977), and had no problem being 13 to 43 in *Coalminer's Daughter*, which won her an Oscar. Naturally she did her own singing, turning out a creditable impersonation of Loretta Lynn's vocal style. Even if the years caught up with her a little for *Missing* (Costa-Gavras, 1982) and *Raggedy Man* (Fisk, 1982), she'll never want for work. She was set designer on films like *Phantom of the Paradise, Death Game*, and *Eraserhead*. And she could always go back to singing.

Sissy Spacek *(b.1949) as Pinky Rose, with Robert Fortier in Robert Altman's* Three Women *(1977); (above) as Loretta Lynn in* Coalminer's Daughter *(Apted, 1980) with Minnie Pearl and Ernest Tubb.*

A contemporary at the Munich drama school was Rainer Werner Fassbinder, and the career of **Hanna Schygulla** became linked with that of the prolific, moody and controversial German film-maker from his earliest productions in 1968 almost until his final work in 1982. Not surprisingly hailed as a new Dietrich-Sternberg partnership for a while, the comparison was misleading; Fassbinder's hard-edged style, with its bleak and startling frankness, had none of Sternberg's romanticism, and Schygulla's open, matter-of-fact sexuality owed nothing to Dietrich innuendo, although in the fishnet stockings of *Lili Marlene* (1981) the reminders were unmistakeable. Her amiably independent air made an intriguing counterpoint to her unscrupulous role as Maria Braun in 1979, and as another Madame Bovary in the beautifully filmed costume drama *Effi Briest*. With performances for Godard, Scola, and Wajda, she is beginning to travel successfully.

Hanna Schygulla (b. 1943) as Rainer Werner Fassbinder's *Effi Briest* (1974).

'You can't be a movie star,' her father said; 'movie stars are beautiful.' From that moment, **Debra Winger** was determined not to be a movie star; she wanted to be an actress. She had worked on a kibbutz, studied sociology, and was nearly paralysed in an accident; now she studied acting, played Wonder Woman's kid sister on television, and won the lead opposite John Travolta in *Urban Cowboy* (Bridges, 1980). Stardom was then difficult to avoid, with Oscar nominations for *An Officer and a Gentleman* in 1981 and for James L. Brooks' *Terms of Endearment* in 1983. She was also part of the voice for E.T., and like him has a long, long way to go.

Fanny Ardant studied political science in London in the early 1970s, was fired from the French Embassy for being an unpunctual secretary, and was one of the most surprising tea-ladies ever to roam the corridors of the B.B.C. Returning to France, she then spent six years in the theatre, contributed to films by Jessua and

Lelouch, and was spotted by Truffaut in a television play. As the violently passionate neighbour to Depardieu in *La Femme d'à Côté*, she had a huge and well-deserved success, and European cinema has been full of her ever since, in films by Delvaux, Resnais, Schlöndorff, and in Truffaut's comedy thriller *Vivement, Dimanche!* (1983).

For her very first film, **Sondra Locke** was nominated for an Oscar; she befriended deaf-mute Alan Arkin in *The Heart is a Lonely Hunter* (Miller, 1968). Similar hits were hard to find, she went reluctantly into television, and had a run of making films that were never released, with Robert Shaw in *A Reflection of Fear* (1973) and with Richard Dreyfuss in *The Second Coming of Suzanne* (1974). Then Clint Eastwood tested her for *Breezy* (1973), cast her in *The Outlaw Josey Wales* (1976), and found her an appealing and compliant partner both off and on screen for five more movies. The interest is understandable.

Debra Winger (b.1955) in *An Officer and a Gentleman* (Hackford, 1981).

Fanny Ardant (b.1949) in François Truffaut's *La Femme d'à Côté* (1980).

Sondra Locke *(b.1947)* in Clint Eastwood's *The Gauntlet* (1977).

Margot Kidder (b. 1948) in *The Amityville Horror* (Rosenberg, 1979).

An original wild child, **Margot Kidder** had wrecked 12 schools by the time she went into modelling and television at 16. You wouldn't think so to see her now as the demure Lois Lane in the *Superman* movies, but she could always make the sparks fly – whether hurling tomatoes at Robert Redford in *The Great Waldo Pepper* (Hill, 1975), or dodging the furniture in *The Amityville Horror* (Rosenberg, 1979). Dynamic and impetuous in films like De Palma's *Sisters* (1972) or *Louisiana* (1984) with Ian Charleson, she's also a film-maker – but promises not to stay off-screen too long.

Stormy 'sex-queen' of the Royal Shakespeare Company from 1967 to 1972, **Helen Mirren** shows few traces these days of her convent upbringing in Southend. After training to be a drama teacher, she took up the stage herself, and was also frequently seen in television plays. The cinema first claimed her at a high cultural level with *A Midsummer Night's Dream* (Hall, 1968) and *Miss Julie* (Phillips/Glenister, 1972), but quickly showed a preference for the more sultry image with roles like *Hussy* (Chapman, 1980). Whether camping it up in *Caligula* (Brass, 1979) or looking elegant in crime thrillers like *The Long Good Friday*, she seldom leaves an audience unscathed.

Helen Mirren (b. 1945) in John McKenzie's *The Long Good Friday* (1980).

PICK
OF THE TOPS

To sum it all up by nominating the best of the greatest is an irresistible but also an impossible task. Even a hit parade of a hundred would be scant courtesy to innumerable other fine actresses of equally affectionate memory. And the list would keep changing all the time. If we settle, however, for an arbitrary fourteen all-time favourites, with mass appeal as the reasonable criterion, and a certain amount of personal prejudice as an *un*reasonable deciding factor, it's possible to identify the following range of faces. It would be no hardship, if one were so inclined, to share one's desert island with these illustrious and well-loved (even, perhaps, ardently hated) symbols of the twentieth century. As long as movies are discussed, they are certainly the faces that will come to mind most frequently. And the films with which they're associated would be adequate entertainment for a lifetime. But tastes and desert islands change, and the Oscar-winners are different every year. So it's a game anyone can play.

Greta Garbo
If the other faces in this brief gallery could be combined, the result would probably have Garbo's features. Disregard the whimsical fish-net, unwise attempt to improve on a masterpiece, and it's a countenance cheeringly at odds with the legend. Nothing distant or dismissive. Just a smile.

Marlene Dietrich
Almost everything that mattered to the Dietrich image is concealed, but the precision and poise are unmistakable. Nobody was her

equal for disappearing into a hat, be it the dissolute topper of *Blue Angel*, the hussar's helmet of *Scarlet Empress*, or the plunge-brimmed nonsense, heavy with

flowers, of *Blonde Venus*. 'Marlene is not Marlene, she is me,' said Sternberg, himself much given to headgear. Maybe so, but on her it all looked much better.

Katharine Hepburn
Looking at her here, just about to fly the Atlantic or catch a leopard or fix the car or something, it's the mouth with its Joan Crawford acreage, generous and determined, that catches the eye. To suggest a link between the 'Godfather' and the girl that she was, the irresistible force she became, may seem fanciful. But when she made an offer, refusal could mean an arm and a leg.

Ingrid Bergman
A favourite memory would be from *Under Capricorn*; in sinuous choreography with Hitchcock's mobile camera, she tells her story of love and loss in a single mesmerizing monologue, no cuts, no tricks, the whole speech right there on the screen. Thirty years later, in the Oscar-winning *Autumn Sonata*, the same skill worked an even subtler magic. One of the cinema's great sufferers, she made no secret that her troubles were of her own making. And that she'd no choice but to carry on making them.

Marilyn Monroe

If she hadn't existed, somebody would have had to invent her. It was Marilyn's misfortune to personify a global fantasy, all good-time promise and tantalizing innocence. Among the pin-ups, knowing all the documented details of her story, it's still hard to see reality. Instead, guilty as we may feel, the film memories – the billowing skirt from *Seven Year Itch*, the all-girls-together wriggle of *Some Like It Hot* – don't help to erase the suspicion that off-screen she was, although a best-seller, pure fiction.

Elizabeth Taylor

Back then, around the time of *Ivanhoe*, she was a stunner. The acting was a help, of course, but it didn't matter too much. One look from those eyes and horsemen fell like corn. But if Marilyn never had enough years, Taylor had too many, in which to become hyper-real, flesh-and-blood in overdrive, excessive with husbands and wealth. And if her acting improved substantially (in *Who's Afraid of Virginia Woolf?*, say, or *Secret Ceremony*), the irony was that we liked her much better the way she used to be.

Vivien Leigh
As cinema legends go, this one's
known by heart. They discovered
her at the last moment and then,
Scarlett or Blanche or Mrs Stone,
the lady stayed the same – fiery,
impulsive, and perpetually hungry.
 In the great, grand context of
Gone With the Wind, rolling
massively through a chronicle of
history in which she was the
merest irrelevance, Scarlett
fought a private Civil War that
completely upstaged the rest of
the nation. She and her kind will
always fight such battles. That's
how movie history is made.

Sophia Loren
It's the lower lip, the touch of sulk. There's a pleasing amplitude about the lot of her, and she laughs so half the town can enjoy the joke, but the lip declares she'll have things her own way. Princess or street-girl, she's the outgoing type, almost not a star at all with hair down and neo-realist washing on the line. It's good to know, thanks to *Two Women*, that she can let rip like Magnani. Otherwise it would be tempting just to idolize her for the looks alone.

Claudia Cardinale
With Claudia, it's the smile, although no-one would ever complain about the rest of her. She has a daunting pout, a hint of severity when contemplating, perhaps, the next move. But the smile unleashes a whole pageant of celebrations, all-encompassing, with an impact that removes the feet from the ground, the heart from the head. Fellini used her quite ruthlessly in *Otto e Mezzo* as the girl of his dreams, and although she smouldered for Visconti the damage was done. A bright, fresh vision of the unattainable, she is more inspiration than actuality, more dream than a dull world deserves.

Audrey Hepburn

The attraction of Audrey is in perpetual youth. She contrives to be the first girl-friend, the one that liked frogs and, from sheer compassion, might test their chances of becoming princes. Her innocence made her the perfect Sabrina, a heart-stopping Natasha, a delectable Eliza. In all her films, the process of growing up has contrived to leave her unrepentant, the easy sophistication no more than a façade from which the eager, incredulous child could burst at any moment, laughing at the joke. The joke is probably on us, but the cinema has been a happier place for her presence in it.

Diane Keaton

She does her best with the chores of keeping house, but she's not inclined to passivity. Sooner or later something snaps, the husbands are bundled out the door, and she's taking another shot at the lonely life. Paranoia hovers behind those restless eyes; all the praise in the world can't persuade her that it's deserved – or even genuine. She's funny, smart and helpless, and wouldn't mind being rescued so long as she can do it herself.

Jean Seberg

The cinema's little-girl-lost, she was abused from the moment they picked her for the stake-out and cut back her hair into startled brevity. The lady was for burning, and as the catastrophes of her life became more brutal, the pain and confusion in her gaze was appalling to see. That they should make a musical in exploitative epitaph to her suicide was sadly in keeping. Like Harlow and Monroe she had a disastrous destiny and there was no way to save her.

Anouk Aimée

Like Claudia, she's self-contained, a degree or two adrift from the mundane, placid under glass as if breathing some private sustenance. Where Dietrich's Lola was out to administer a demolition job, Anouk's, with the same top hat and thighs, was a demonstration of detachment. The gentle, melancholy smile seems to invite offers of sympathy and support, but pursue her, even in humble worship, and she'd disperse in a mist. Like Garbo, she seems content to let the world spin without her. Such serenity carries an eternal fascination.

Monica Vitti
And Monica too is nobody's property, although all compliments are gracefully received. Antonioni made her a star in roles of distraught resignation, but the sense of comedy kept peeping through, and at her happiest in her later films she's mugging away to her heart's content. As seen here, coping with Delon in _The Eclipse_, she's the actress one would most like to take home to shock the parents witless, but she vowed at 12 she'd never marry and it's probably as well. The cinema's the place for dreaming, after all.

Index

Note Page references in **heavy type** refer to main entries, in *italics* to illustrations.